GCSE RELIGIOUS STUDIES
FOR EDEXCEL A — UNIT 16

MARK'S GOSPEL

endorsed by
edexcel

INA TAYLOR

OXFORD
UNIVERSITY PRESS

OXFORD
UNIVERSITY PRESS

Great Clarendon Street, Oxford OX2 6DP

Oxford University Press is a department of the University of Oxford. It furthers the University's objective of excellence in research, scholarship,and education by publishing worldwide in

Oxford   New York

Auckland Cape Town Dar es Salaam Hong Kong Karachi
Kuala Lumpur Madrid Melbourne Mexico City Nairobi
New Delhi Shanghai Taipei Toronto

With offices in

Argentina Austria Brazil Chile Czech Republic France Greece
Guatemala Hungary Italy Japan Poland Portugal Singapore
South Korea Switzerland Thailand Turkey Ukraine Vietnam

Oxford is a registered trade mark of Oxford University Press
in the UK and in certain other countries

© Ina Taylor 2010

The moral rights of the author have been asserted

Database right Oxford University Press (maker)

First published 2010

British Library Cataloguing in Publication Data

Data available

ISBN 978-1-85008-561-4

FD5614

10 9 8 7 6

Printed in Malaysia by Vivar Printing Sdn Bhd.

Paper used in the production of this book is a natural, recyclable product made from wood grown in sustainable forests. The manufacturing process conforms to the environmental regulations of the country of origin.

Acknowledgements

p.8–9 © iStockphoto.com/concept mediaworks/; p.10 © iStockphoto.com/concept mediaworks/; p.11 © iStockphoto.com/Rockfinder Photography; p.12 © Pontino/Alamy; p.13 © Alamy/Joe Fox; p.16 © iStockphoto.com/RonTech2000; p.17 © Mike Goldwater/Alamy; p.18 © Tim Graham/Alamy; p.19 © Gareth Fuller/PA Wire/Press Association Images; p.20 Jenny © Fotolia; p.21 © Brian O'Sullivan/EMPICS Entertainment; p.22 © Courtesy of Ina Taylor; p.23 © Sipa Press/Rex Features; p.26 © iStockphoto.com/Konstantin Papadakis; p.27 John Reilly/The Healing of the Lunatic Boy from the Methodist Church Collection of Modern Christian Art Copyright: Trustess for Methodist Church Purposes, used by permission the Trustees of the Collection; p.28 2010 Huiping Zhu. Image from Bigstock.com.; p.30 © Jochen Tack/Alamy; p.31 © Peter Cavanagh/Alamy; p.32 © Francis Dean/Rex Features; p.33 Lo Spagna, The Agony in the Garden, bought 1878, © Copyright The National Gallery 2010; p.34 © iStockphoto.com/Nils Kahle; p.35 © Gregory Wrona/Alamy; p.38–39 © The Art Archive/Alamy; p.40 © Courtesy of Ina Taylor; p.41 © Yves Gellie/Corbis; p.42 © iStockphoto.com/Elena Elisseeva; p.43 © Colin Underhill/Alamy; p.45 © mediablitzimages (uk) Limited/Alamy; p.48 2010 Paul Cummings. Image from Bigstock.com.; p.49 Churches Advertising Network, www.churchads.org.uk; p.50 2010 Tan Kian Khoon. Image from Bigstock.com.; p.51 © isifa Image Service s.r.o./Alamy; p.52 © David Noble Photography/Alamy; p.53 © iStockphoto.com/Steven Allan; p.58 © PjrStudio/Alamy; p.59 Courtesy of the Peace Tax Seven; p.60 © Stephen Lloyd UK/Alamy; p.62 © Nic Cleave Photography/Alamy; p.63 © Jack Picone/Alamy; p.64 © The Art Archive/Alamy; p.68–69 2010 Colin Horner. Image from Bigstock.com.; p.70 © iStockphoto.com/Leonid Nyshko; p.71 (top) © Courtesy of Ina Taylor, (bottom) © iStockphoto.com/Jill Battaglia; p.72 © Art Directors; p.74 2010 Colin Horner. Image from Bigstock.com.; p.76 Kenneth Garrett/National Geographic Stock; p.77 Ugolino di Nerio, The Betrayal of Christ, bought 1885, © Copyright The National Gallery 2010; p.80 © Art Directors & TRIP/Alamy; p.81 © ACAT UK; p.82 © Israel images/Alamy; p.83 © Courtesy of Ina Taylor; p.85 © Courtesy of Ina Taylor; p.86 © The Gallery Collection/Corbis; p.87 William Roberts/The Crucifixion from the Methodist Church Collection of Modern Christian Art Copyright: Trustess for Methodist Church Purposes, used by permission the Trustees of the Collection; p.90 © iStockphoto.com/Glenda Powers; p.91 © Courtesy of Ina Taylor; p.92 © Courtesy of Ina Taylor; p.93 Rick Sargeant © Fotolia; p.94 © Courtesy of Ina Taylor; p.95 © PA/PA Archive/Press Association Images; p.98–99 © D Core Ocean/Alamy; p.100 © Keith McIntyre/Alamy; p.101 © Israel images/Alamy; p.103 (top) © Eddie Gerald/Alamy, (bottom) © iStockphoto.com/pixhook; p.104 © Hemis/Alamy; p.108 © D Core Ocean/Alamy; p.109 Eularia Clarke/Storm Over the Lake from the Methodist Church Collection of Modern Christian Art Copyright: Trustess for Methodist Church Purposes, used by permission the Trustees of the Collection; p.110 © Ivan Sekretarev/AP/Press Association Images; p.111 Eularia Clarke/The Five Thousand from the Methodist Church Collection of Modern Christian Art Copyright: Trustess for Methodist Church Purposes, used by permission the Trustees of the Collection; p.112 © Mary Evans Picture Library/Douglas McCarthy; p.113 © Joe McDonald/CORBIS; p.115 © iStockphoto.com/Anatolii Tsekhmister; p.117 © Mary Evans Picture Library/Alamy; p.121 © iStockphoto.com/irakite; p.123 Jan Mostaert, Christ Crowned With Thorns, presented by Henry Wagner 1924, © Copyright The National Gallery 2010; p.124 2010 Zhang Zhenghua. Image from Bigstock.com.; p.125 © Mary Evans Picture Library/Alamy

Scripture quotations taken from *The Holy Bible, New International Version Anglicised* copyright © 1979, 1984 by International Bible Society. Used by permission of Hodder & Stoughton Publishers, a division of Hodder Headline Ltd. All rights reserved. "NIV" is a registered trademark of International Bible Society. UK trademark number 1448790.

This material has been endorsed by Edexcel and offers high quality support for the delivery of Edexcel qualifications.

Edexcel endorsement does not mean that this material is essential to achieve any Edexcel qualification, nor does it mean that this is the only suitable material available to support any Edexcel qualification. No endorsed material will be used verbatim in setting any Edexcel examination and any resource lists produced by Edexcel shall include this and other appropriate texts. While this material has been through an Edexcel quality assurance process, all responsibility for the content remains with the publisher.

Copies of official specifications for all Edexcel qualifications may be found on the Edexcel website – www.edexcel.com

Editor: Judi Hunter, Spellbound Books

Text design: eMC Design Ltd., www.emcdesign.org.uk

Layout: Rosa Capacchione

Picture researcher: Cathy Hurren

Illustrator: Rory Walker

Cover design: Form, www.form.uk.com

Cover image: © Lincoln Rogers

Every effort has been made to contact copyright holders of material used in this publication. If any copyright holder has been overlooked, we will be pleased to make any necessary arrangements.

Contents

Introduction

Some helpful tips about using this book

This textbook is designed to help you prepare for the Edexcel exam *Mark's Gospel*. The exam requires you to study the nature of St Mark's Gospel and its effects on the lives of Christians in the UK. This book offers you plenty of up-to-date material on the way Christians today approach the accounts in Mark's Gospel. Half of the course and the exam focus on learning and understanding what St Mark was telling his readers about events in Jesus' life and what he understood they meant. The other half of the course challenges you to think about these accounts for yourself and come to your own informed opinion about the significance of them, as well as the way Christians today might interpret the information. Your own response to the material in Mark's Gospel can be religious or non-religious; what the examiner is marking is whether you can argue the case you make and support it with evidence.

How does the book work?

The book has been designed to follow the exam specification very closely. It is divided into four chapters covering the sections you are required to study.

Chapter 1 Discipleship

This chapter examines different facets of discipleship. It looks at the sort of people Jesus chose and what he told them about the job they were going to do. You will study the cost of discipleship in terms of family relationships, personal wealth and status, and will look at the problems of discipleship and the way in which the Twelve failed Jesus at different times, even to the extent of running away when he needed them most. Some of the aspects of discipleship are studied through parables, others through events in Jesus' life. In each case, you will consider the implications for Christians today and the problems discipleship might cause them.

Chapter 2 Conflict and argument

In this chapter you will study the way in which Jesus' ministry brought him into conflict with the Jewish religious authorities. It will include examining a healing miracle, as well as some of the religious questions Jewish scholars confronted Jesus with as they tried to trick him into committing blasphemy. You will think about the arguments Jesus gave and see the way tension built up between Jesus and the Temple authorities. These issues will be examined with Christians today in mind, especially their significance for social and community cohesion in modern Britain.

Chapter 3 Death and resurrection

In this chapter you will study in detail the final week of Jesus' life. You will consider the meaning of the Last Supper, the prayers in Gethsemane, Jesus' betrayal and arrest, as well as the two trials. Jesus' crucifixion, burial and resurrection are examined in detail in order to understand their importance for Christians today. You will look at what Mark wrote and think about the way Christians today might react to these accounts.

Chapter 4 The identity of Jesus — in otha religions

In this chapter you will think about who Mark thought Jesus was, who people at the time believed he was, as well as modern Christians' understanding of Jesus' identity. This will involve examining some significant events in Jesus' life, such as his baptism and transfiguration, then considering how Christians today understand these events. There will be a close consideration of the miracles: what Mark thought they showed about Jesus and the problems these extraordinary events pose for modern Christians. You will also examine the titles given to Jesus and what they tell Christians about his identity.

→ Islam, Hinduism, Judaism etc :

Topic pages

The pages have been designed with lots of features to make learning each topic lively and memorable.

Keywords

Each chapter contains 12 keywords. These appear on the opening pages of each chapter, throughout the chapter, and are collected in the back of the book, in a Keyword glossary.

Bible quotations

Highlighted phrases and detailed commentary boxes help to make sense of what is going on in the Bible passages from Mark's Gospel.

Activities

The activities reinforce your learning. You can work on them individually or tackle them as a class.

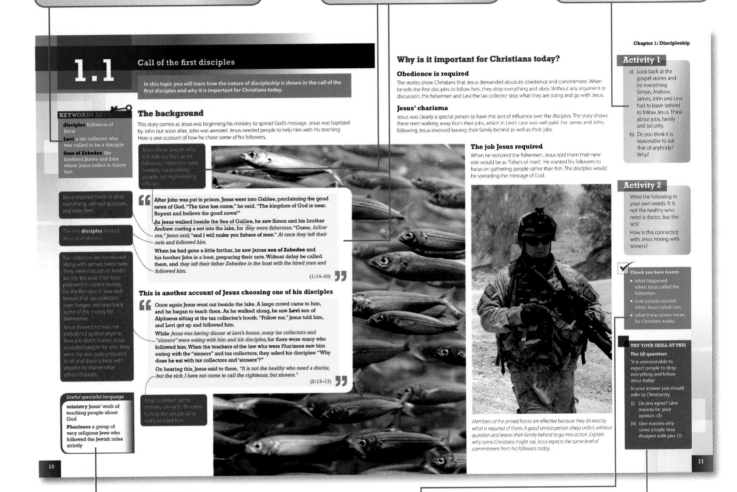

Useful specialist language

You will not be asked to give the meaning of these words, but you can boost your marks by using them correctly in your exam answers.

Check you have learnt

This asks you to summarize what you have learnt about each topic, so you can check you've grasped the key points.

Try your skill at this

These questions will give you an opportunity to practise your newly learnt skills with exam-style questions, building up your knowledge and confidence.

Giving you plenty of coaching

In order to help you get the best possible grades that you can, there is plenty of help with improving your exam skills. Within every chapter of study there are three Skills Coaching spreads. These are designed to help you become familiar with the four different types of questions you will see on the exam paper.

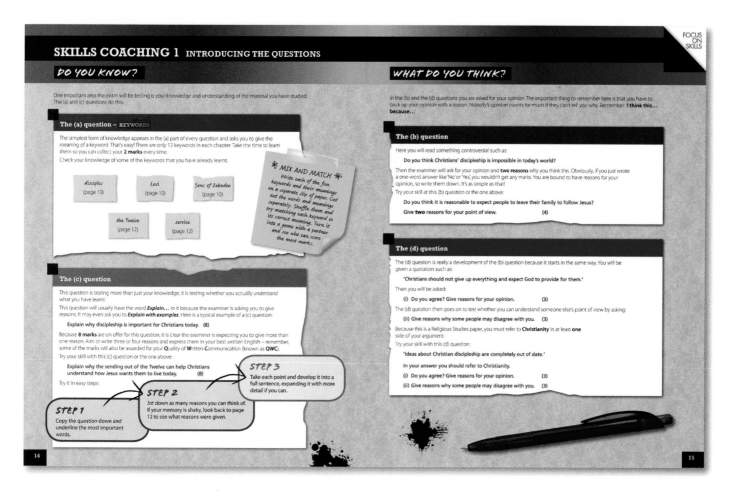

The left-hand page is called 'Do you know?' because it concentrates on the two questions that test your knowledge and understanding of what you have learnt. This skill carries half the marks. The right-hand page is called 'What do you think?' because it helps you to give your views and reasons. These two questions carry the other half of the marks on the paper.

There will be analysis of the questions so you get used to understanding exactly what the examiner is looking for. You will also look closely at the way the examiner marks each type of question with examples of the marking grids that are used. For each type of question, you will get step-by-step help with constructing an answer plus a few chances to 'Be the examiner' yourself. On these occasions you will be reading someone else's answer, comparing it with the marking criteria, and then awarding a grade and giving the student a few tips on improving their marks!

Each End of Chapter Check reminds you of what you should have learnt in that chapter and contains a practice exam page for you to try out.

This is a very exciting course of study with plenty of material to grab your attention and get you arguing. Enjoy!

CHAPTER 1

Discipleship

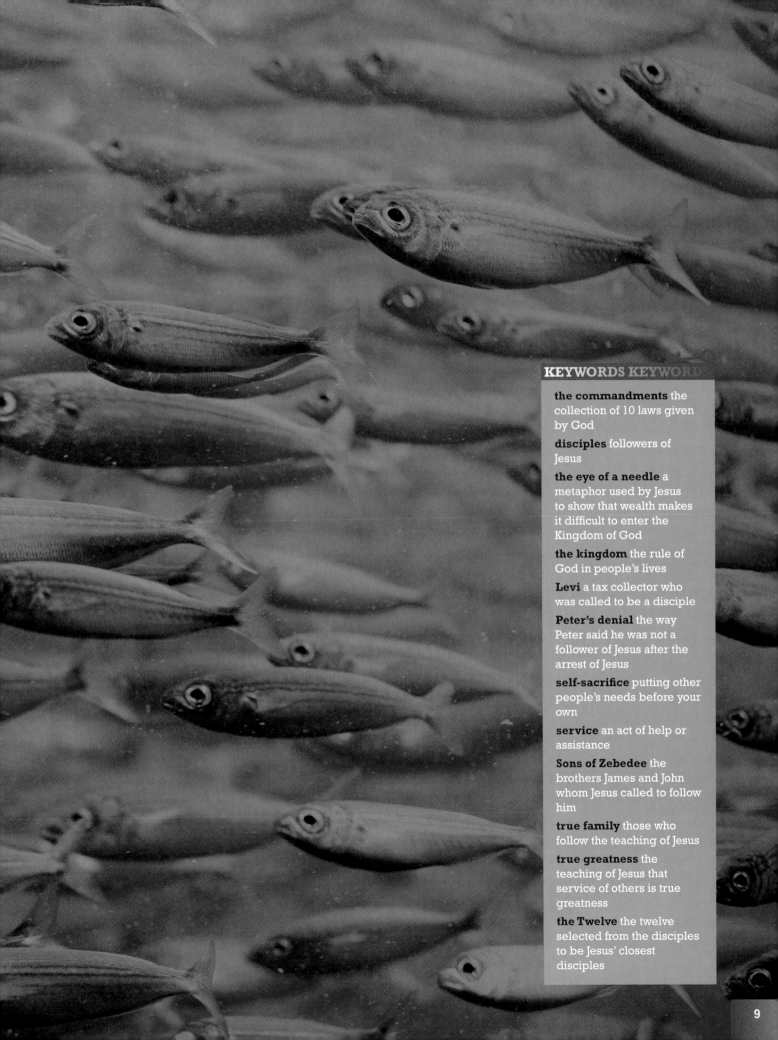

Call of the first disciples

In this topic you will learn how the nature of discipleship is shown in the call of the first disciples and why it is important for Christians today.

KEYWORDS KEYWORD

disciples followers of Jesus

Levi a tax collector who was called to be a disciple

Sons of Zebedee the brothers James and John whom Jesus called to follow him

The background

This story comes as Jesus was beginning his ministry to spread God's message. Jesus was baptized by John but soon after, John was arrested. Jesus needed people to help him with his teaching. Here is one account of how he chose some of his followers.

Jesus chose people who led ordinary lives, as his followers. Fishermen were humble, hardworking people, not high-ranking officials.

Jesus required them to drop everything, without question, and obey him.

The first **disciples** trusted Jesus and obeyed.

> After John was put in prison, Jesus went into Galilee, proclaiming the good news of God. "The time has come," he said. "The kingdom of God is near. Repent and believe the good news!"
>
> As Jesus walked beside the Sea of Galilee, he saw Simon and his brother Andrew casting a net into the lake, for *they were fishermen.* "Come, *follow me," Jesus said,* "and I will make you fishers of men." *At once they left their nets and followed him.*
>
> When he had gone a little farther, he saw James **son of Zebedee** and his brother John in a boat, preparing their nets. Without delay he called them, and *they left their father Zebedee in the boat with the hired men and followed him.*
>
> (1:14–20)

Tax collectors are mentioned along with sinners twice here. They were outcasts in Jewish society because they were prepared to collect money for the Romans. It was well known that tax collectors overcharged and kept back some of the money for themselves.

Jesus showed he was not prejudiced against anyone; their job didn't matter. Jesus accepted people for who they were. He was quite prepared to sit and share a meal with anyone no matter what others thought.

This is another account of Jesus choosing one of his disciples

> Once again Jesus went out beside the lake. A large crowd came to him, and he began to teach them. As he walked along, he saw **Levi** son of Alphaeus sitting at the tax collector's booth. "Follow me," Jesus told him, and Levi got up and followed him.
>
> While *Jesus was having dinner at Levi's house, many tax collectors and "sinners" were eating with him and his disciples,* for there were many who followed him. When the teachers of the law who were Pharisees saw him eating with the "sinners" and tax collectors, they asked his disciples: "Why does he eat with tax collectors and 'sinners'?"
>
> On hearing this, Jesus said to them, *"It is not the healthy who need a doctor, but the sick. I have not come to call the righteous, but sinners."*
>
> (2:13–17)

Useful specialist language

ministry Jesus' work of teaching people about God

Pharisees a group of very religious Jews who followed the Jewish rules strictly

Jesus summed up his ministry on earth: he came to help the people who really needed him.

Why is it important for Christians today?

Obedience is required

The stories show Christians that Jesus demanded absolute obedience and commitment. When he tells the first disciples to follow him, they drop everything and obey. Without any argument or discussion, the fishermen and Levi the tax collector stop what they are doing and go with Jesus.

Jesus' charisma

Jesus was clearly a special person to have this sort of influence over the disciples. The story shows these men walking away from their jobs, which in Levi's case was well-paid. For James and John, following Jesus involved leaving their family behind as well as their jobs.

The job Jesus required

When he recruited the fishermen, Jesus told them their new role would be as "fishers of men". He wanted his followers to focus on gathering people rather than fish. The disciples would be spreading the message of God.

Members of the armed forces are effective because they do exactly what is required of them. A good service person obeys orders without question and leaves their family behind to go into action. Explain why some Christians might say Jesus expects the same level of commitment from his followers today.

Activity 1

a) Look back at the gospel stories and list everything Simon, Andrew, James, John and Levi had to leave behind to follow Jesus. Think about jobs, family and security.

b) Do you think it is reasonable to ask that of anybody? Why?

Activity 2

Write the following in your own words: 'It is not the healthy who need a doctor, but the sick'.

How is this connected with Jesus mixing with sinners?

✓ **Check you have learnt:**

- what happened when Jesus called the fishermen
- how people reacted when Jesus called Levi
- what these stories mean for Christians today.

TRY YOUR SKILL AT THIS

The (d) question:

'It is unreasonable to expect people to drop everything and follow Jesus today.'

In your answer you should refer to Christianity.

(i) Do you agree? Give reasons for your opinion. (3)

(ii) Give reasons why some people may disagree with you. (3)

1.2 Sending out the Twelve disciples

In this topic you will study how the nature of discipleship is shown in the sending out of the Twelve and how it affects ideas about Christian living today.

The background

After Jesus called 12 people to be his closest followers, the men accompanied him on his travels. They learnt how to do the job Jesus had chosen them for by copying their master. When Jesus judged they were ready, he sent them out in pairs. The following passage explains how Jesus wanted them to behave.

> Then Jesus went around teaching from village to village. Calling **the Twelve** to him, he sent them out **two by two** and gave them authority over evil spirits.
>
> These were his instructions: "*Take nothing for the journey except a staff – no bread, no bag, no money in your belts. Wear sandals but not an extra tunic. Whenever you enter a house, stay there until you leave that town. And if any place will not welcome you or listen to you, shake the dust off your feet when you leave, as a testimony against them.*"
>
> They went out *and preached that people should repent. They drove out many demons and anointed many sick people with oil and healed them.*
>
> **(6:7–13)**

Jesus sent his disciples out in pairs for their safety and in order to assist each other with the work he had asked them to do.

Jesus told his disciples not to worry about personal possessions. They took basic things like a walking stick and sandals and trusted in God to provide all that was necessary.

The disciples were told to accept the first hospitality that was offered to them.

The disciples were told not to force their message on people. They preached to those who wanted to hear, but did not have confrontations with people who rejected their message.

The disciples had two jobs: to pass on Jesus' teachings and urge people to repent; and to help people by healing them.

+ HE SHALL COME AGAIN WITH GLORY TO JUDGE BOTH THE LIVING AND THE DEAD + OF HIS KINGD

What were the disciples told to do?

In this passage, Jesus set out very clear rules about how he wanted his closest followers to behave when they were working for him. He asked them to do exactly what he did: preach the word of God that told people to repent and help people. That help often took the form of healing. Sometimes it involved healing the body and other times healing the mind (mental health problems), which is what Mark was referring to when he wrote of power over demons and evil spirits.

The guidelines Jesus laid down for the Twelve, his specially chosen followers, were very testing even for those days. By telling them not to pack clothes, food or money, Jesus was asking them to put their trust totally in God and to accept any hospitality that was offered them. The bag Jesus told them to leave behind would have been one for holding gifts of money or food. This showed that Jesus did not want his followers to accept payment for serving him. He permitted them to accept basic bed and breakfast, if it was offered, but nothing else because they were not doing Jesus' work to make a profit.

Do you think Jesus' instructions to the Twelve have any relevance to this man?

The instruction not to take spare clothes with them meant that Jesus intended the Twelve to travel light. This meant they could move on easily and take their message to as many people as possible.

What does this mean for Christians today?

The instructions Jesus gave to the Twelve when he sent them out on a mission to do his work are relevant to Christians today who go out on missionary work. They understand that it is their job as followers of Jesus to teach his message of repentance and to care for people. This care often takes the form of medical assistance.

Not all Christians today feel that they are called to do missionary work for Jesus by travelling overseas to preach, but they do believe that the ground rules he laid down matter in their journey through life. Christians often take the opportunity to spread God's word in their daily life, not necessarily by preaching but by setting an example of how to live. In the gospel passage, Jesus told the disciples not to be distracted from their task by lengthy preparations, personal possessions or getting into conflict with those who disagreed with them. The message is to concentrate fully on **service** to others as Jesus did.

These men have just been ordained as priests. Which parts of Jesus' instructions to the Twelve do you think are relevant to their future?

DO YOU KNOW?

One important area the exam will be testing is your knowledge and understanding of the material you have studied. The (a) and (c) questions do this.

The (a) question – KEYWORDS

The simplest form of knowledge appears in the (a) part of every question and asks you to give the meaning of a keyword. That's easy! There are only 12 keywords in each chapter. Take the time to learn them so you can collect your **2 marks** every time.

Check your knowledge of some of the keywords that you have already learnt:

> disciples
> (page 10)

> Levi
> (page 10)

> Sons of Zebedee
> (page 10)

> the Twelve
> (page 12)

> service
> (page 12)

> ✳ MIX AND MATCH ✳
> Write each of the five keywords and their meanings on a separate slip of paper. Cut out the words and meanings separately. Shuffle them and try matching each keyword to its correct meaning. Turn it into a game with a partner and see who can score the most marks.

The (c) question

This question is testing more than just your knowledge; it is testing whether you actually *understand* what you have learnt.

This question will usually have the word **Explain...** in it because the examiner is asking you to give reasons. It may even ask you to **Explain with examples**. Here is a typical example of a (c) question:

> Explain why discipleship is important for Christians today.   (8)

Because **8 marks** are on offer for this question, it is clear the examiner is expecting you to give more than one reason. Aim to write three or four reasons and express them in your best written English – remember, some of the marks will also be awarded for your **Q**uality of **W**ritten **C**ommunication (known as **QWC**).

Try your skill with this (c) question or the one above:

> Explain why the sending out of the Twelve can help Christians understand how Jesus wants them to live today.   (8)

Try it in easy steps:

STEP 3

Take each point and develop it into a full sentence, expanding it with more detail if you can.

STEP 2

Jot down as many reasons you can think of. If your memory is shaky, look back to page 12 to see what reasons were given.

STEP 1

Copy the question down and underline the most important words.

In Section 1, there will be an extra 4 marks awarded across all questions for accurate spelling, punctuation and grammar.

WHAT DO YOU THINK?

In the (b) and the (d) questions you are asked for your opinion. The important thing to remember here is that you have to back up your opinion with a reason. Nobody's opinion counts for much if they can't tell you why. Remember: '**I think this… because…**'

The (b) question

Here you will read something controversial such as:

> Do you think Christians' discipleship is impossible in today's world?

Then the examiner will ask for your opinion and **two reasons** why you think this. Obviously, if you just wrote a one-word answer like 'No' or 'Yes', you wouldn't get any marks. You are bound to have reasons for your opinion, so write them down. It's as simple as that!

Try your skill at this (b) question or the one above:

> Do you think it is reasonable to expect people to leave their family to follow Jesus?
>
> Give **two** reasons for your point of view.   (4)

The (d) question

The (d) question is really a development of the (b) question because it starts in the same way. You will be given a quotation such as:

> 'Christians should not give up everything and expect God to provide for them.'

Then you will be asked:

> (i) Do you agree? Give reasons for your opinion.   (3)

The (d) question then goes on to test whether you can understand someone else's point of view by asking:

> (ii) Give reasons why some people may disagree with you.   (3)

Because this is a Religious Studies paper, you must refer to **Christianity** in at least **one** side of your argument.

Try your skill with this (d) question:

> 'Ideas about Christian discipleship are completely out of date.'
>
> In your answer you should refer to Christianity.
>
> (i) Do you agree? Give reasons for your opinion.   (3)
>
> (ii) Give reasons why some people may disagree with you.   (3)

1.3 The true family of Jesus

In this topic you will examine how the costs of discipleship are shown in the true family of Jesus and why this teaching causes problems for some Christians today.

KEYWORDS KEYWORD

true family those who follow the teaching of Jesus

The background

Jesus' healings and preaching attracted such large crowds that he went away up a hill to find quiet and name his 12 followers. When he returned home, he found hordes of people waiting to hear him. Instead of sitting down to a meal, Jesus began teaching them. Mark tells us that Jesus' family heard about this and arrived 'to take charge of him' because they had been told that Jesus must be mad.

> *Then Jesus' mother and brothers arrived.* **Standing outside, they sent someone in to call him. A crowd was sitting around him, and they told him, "Your mother and brothers are outside looking for you."**
>
> *"Who are my mother and my brothers?" he asked.*
>
> **Then he looked at those seated in a circle around him and said,** *"Here are my mother and my brothers! Whoever does God's will is my brother and sister and mother."*
>
> **(3:31–35)**

Jesus had brothers and sisters, but since Mary was a virgin when Jesus was born they were his half-brothers and half-sisters with Joseph as their father.

Those listening to Jesus were shocked that he did not obey his family's request to go and see them.

Jesus seemed to disregard his relatives, but in fact he was opening up family membership. Everyone can belong to God's family if they do God's will.

Activity 1

Script or role play a conversation between a Christian teenager who has volunteered to spend Christmas helping at a drop-in centre for the homeless and his aunt who thinks he should spend Christmas with the family.

Activity 2

In modern Britain, it is considered acceptable for families to put their elderly relatives in a care home and pay someone to look after them. People in some cultures believe we should care for our elderly parents at home because they cared for us in childhood.

List the points each side would make to support their case.

Some of Jesus' followers today believe that they should put aside their own relations and devote their love and attention to caring for those with no family to turn to. Explain who you think should have first call on your time and attention: a starving family in the developing world, or someone in your own family who is going through a hard time.

Why does this teaching cause problems for some Christians today?

Some Christians point to one of the Ten Commandments which states, 'Respect your father and mother'. The problem is that Jesus appeared to break this by not obeying his mother's request to go out and see her. However, other Christians would say that Jesus put the command to love God above all others and to love your neighbours next.

Is blood thicker than water?

This is a well-known saying that some people use because they believe we owe more to our biological family (our blood relatives – although families can be made up of people who are not related to us by blood but whom we consider to be our family) than we do to anybody else. Our family is always there for us no matter what we do. Brothers and sisters usually 'look out' for each other at school or on the street. It is the sort of loyalty that exists between family members; everyone cares for each other.

Jesus' teaching causes some Christians problems because he seems to set aside the strong bond of family life that is central to Christian marriage. Some say Jesus is not denying the power of family attachments but offering the same love to all of his followers: the bond between God's followers, the **true family**, will be an even stronger bond than the one between blood relatives. Some might say this is unrealistic.

✓ **Check you have learnt:**

- what happened when Jesus' family asked him to join them
- what Jesus meant by his true family
- two reasons why this teaching might cause Christians problems.

TRY YOUR SKILL AT THIS

The (c) question:

Explain why Jesus' teachings about the family might cause problems for some Christians today. (8)

What is true greatness?

In this topic you will examine how the costs of discipleship are shown in true greatness and why this teaching causes problems for some Christians today.

KEYWORDS KEYWORD

self-sacrifice putting other people's needs before your own

true greatness the teaching of Jesus that service of others is true greatness

The disciples were shown to be ordinary human beings despite the fact that they were chosen by Jesus to do great things. They squabbled over who was more important than the other. It is possible that they were arguing about who would become leader after Jesus' death.

Jesus turned their ideas of importance upside down by explaining that the greatest person is the one who makes no effort to push themselves forward. The person who cares for others' needs before their own is the greatest.

Jesus chose a small child as the least important person in Jewish society because they have no rights. The one who cares for the least important person shows they really understand Jesus' message.

Jesus told his disciples that he is the Son of God. Those who accepted Jesus were accepting God into their lives.

The background

The disciples had just witnessed a healing miracle (see page 26) and heard Jesus preach. As they were walking away, Jesus told them that he would be handed over to his enemies, be killed and then rise again. The disciples did not understand what Jesus was talking about and were afraid to ask for an explanation. Instead, they passed the time as they walked, arguing amongst themselves.

> They came to Capernaum. When he was in the house, he asked them, "What were you arguing about on the road?" But they kept quiet because on the way *they had argued about who was the greatest.*
>
> Sitting down, Jesus called the Twelve and said, *"If anyone wants to be first, he must be the very last, and the servant of all."*
>
> He took a little child and had him stand among them. Taking him in his arms, he said to them, *"Whoever welcomes one of these little children in my name welcomes me*; and *whoever welcomes me does not welcome me but the one who sent me."*
>
> (9:33–37)

Why does this teaching cause problems for Christians today?

Jesus' disciples found his teaching quite revolutionary for their time and Christians today still find his teachings difficult to cope with. In today's society, the quiet person who gets on with their job and doesn't push themselves forward is often ignored. Ambition is something that is applauded in the twenty-first century. Few people choose the quiet person to be the leader, no matter how good they are at their job.

Jesus' teaching raises a lot of problems for modern Christians. He was saying that **true greatness** comes from being the servant of others. People in the twenty-first century rarely see humbleness as a virtue, though many do admire aid workers who travel to disaster zones to help the destitute and wounded.

I don't want to be treated as a doormat!

Some Christians fear that if they act as a servant to others, as Jesus required, they will be taken for granted. They find it very hard to believe that behaving in such a lowly way will achieve anything worthwhile. Perhaps Jesus' message was that his disciples should be more concerned about what God thinks of their behaviour rather than how people on earth judge them. For many Christians in today's society, this is a hard lesson to learn.

For some Christians, the late Mother Teresa was an example of Christian discipleship. She lived a life of complete **self-sacrifice** because she left behind her family and friends and went to work in the slums in Calcutta. There, she tended the diseased and the dying who had been abandoned by everybody else. Which quotation from Mark 9:33–37 would make an ideal caption for this picture? Why?

Activity 1

Use the passage from Mark's Gospel to explain what Jesus meant by true greatness.

Activity 2

Try learning the quotation: "If anyone wants to be first, he must be the very last, and the servant of all" by heart. If you find this tricky, learn the gist of it to use in an answer. What does this quotation mean to a Christian?

The leader of the Anglican Church is the Archbishop of Canterbury. Christians expect him to lead from the front and to be outspoken in the media if there are issues of concern. Why is a role such as his likely to cause problems for some Christians today?

 Check you have learnt:

- what Christians mean by 'the first shall be last'
- what Jesus taught about true greatness
- two reasons why Christians today find this teaching a problem.

TRY YOUR SKILL AT THIS

The (b) question:

Do you think it is possible to be a great leader if you don't push yourself forward?

Give **two** reasons for your point of view. (4)

The problems of being rich

In this topic you will examine how the costs of discipleship are shown in the rich man and why this teaching causes problems for some Christians today.

The background

When Jesus finished teaching the huge crowds some people brought their children to him to be blessed. The disciples protested and Jesus was angry, saying that the kingdom of heaven belonged to such lowly ones as these. It was at this point that the rich young man appeared with his question.

> As Jesus started on his way, a man ran up to him and fell on his knees before him. "Good teacher," he asked, "what must I do to inherit eternal life?"
>
> "Why do you call me good?" Jesus answered. "No one is good – except God alone. *You know **the commandments**: 'Do not murder, do not commit adultery, do not steal, do not give false testimony, do not defraud, honour your father and mother.'"*
>
> "Teacher," he declared, "all these I have kept since I was a boy."
>
> Jesus looked at him and loved him. "One thing you lack," he said. *"Go, sell everything you have and give to the poor, and you will have treasure in heaven. Then come, follow me."*
>
> At this the man's face fell. He went away sad, because he had great wealth.
>
> Jesus looked around and said to his disciples, *"How hard it is for the rich to enter the kingdom of God!"*
>
> The disciples were amazed at his words. But Jesus said again, "Children, how hard it is to enter the kingdom of God! *It is easier for a camel to go through **the eye of a needle** than for a rich man to enter the kingdom of God."*
>
> The disciples were even more amazed, and said to each other, "Who then can be saved?"
>
> Jesus looked at them and said, *"With man this is impossible, but not with God; all things are possible with God."*
>
> Peter said to him, "We have left everything to follow you!"
>
> *"I tell you the truth,"* Jesus replied, *"no one who has left home or brothers or sisters or mother or father or children or fields for me and the gospel will fail to receive a hundred times as much in this present age (homes, brothers, sisters, mothers, children and fields – and with them, persecutions) and in the age to come, eternal life. But many who are first will be last, and the last first."*
>
> (10:17–31) ""

The commandments were the Ten Commandments God gave to Moses, which set out the rules of everyday Jewish life.

The price of discipleship was to give up everything, which meant wealth for this man.

Jesus acknowledged that riches can be a barrier to reaching God.

Jesus used the image of a camel finding it impossible to squeeze through a needle's eye to show the impossibility of a rich person entering heaven.

Jesus reassured his followers that they were not on their own. God will help people.

Jesus told his disciples that God will repay their sacrifices many times over in heaven.

This is the same idea as expressed on page 18, of God's world turning things upside down.

What point was Jesus making?

Jesus told his followers to focus on what really mattered and not be carried away by earthly things like their job, family or possessions. God demands more than just obeying set rules. Jesus knew this was asking a lot of people, but he reassured them that, no matter how difficult it was, God would help them and the great rewards would be worth the effort.

Why do these teachings about wealth cause problems for some Christians today?

For many Christians, this particular teaching shows the gulf between Jesus' world in first-century Palestine and ours in the twenty-first century. They argue that it would have been much easier for Jesus and his disciples to lead a simple life without possessions or money than it is for us. In our society, it would be thought of as wrong to give everything away, lead a wandering life and assume others will supply our basic needs. To many people, this is totally irresponsible.

The teachings also cause some Christians to wonder if anyone with money and possessions will be able to get to heaven. Many modern Christians believe that having lots of money is not the issue, it is the good that the money is put towards which matters.

This is the daughter of millionaire celebrity Sir Bob Geldof. Do you think Peaches Geldof would find it harder than most of us to lead a simple life? Why?

1.6

The parable of the tenants

In this topic you will examine how the costs of discipleship are shown in the parable of the tenants and the story's relationship to Christians today.

Useful specialist language

parable a story Jesus told to help his followers understand his teachings; all parts of these stories have a deeper meaning

capstone a stone that crowns the top of a construction, sometimes referred to as a 'cornerstone'; it is a vital support in a building

The background

This story comes at a time when the success of Jesus' ministry was beginning to annoy the Jewish authorities. They stood around listening to what Jesus had to say, ready to take advantage of any opportunity to arrest him. Jesus often used parables in his teaching to enable people to understand the stories at different levels.

Jesus knew his teachings would be easier for people to understand if they were in the form of a story with various layers of meaning for people to think about.

At the time of Jesus' baptism, God said, "You are my Son, whom I love; with you I am well pleased" (see page 100).

Jesus predicted his crucifixion at the hands of those he had come to save.

Jesus told his listeners that God would return to take vengeance on those who had killed his son and his messengers.

The capstone is the stone that crowns the building. Those on earth may reject people as unimportant, but God can see their real worth and will raise them to a high position in heaven.

The Jewish leaders understood the parable was about them and they looked for a way to silence Jesus.

> *He then began to speak to them in parables*: "A man planted a vineyard. He put a wall around it, dug a pit for the winepress and built a watchtower. Then he rented the vineyard to some farmers and went away on a journey. At harvest time he sent a servant to the tenants to collect from them some of the fruit of the vineyard. But they seized him, beat him and sent him away empty-handed. Then he sent another servant to them; they struck this man on the head and treated him shamefully. He sent still another, and that one they killed. He sent many others; some of them they beat, others they killed.
>
> *"He had one left to send, a son, whom he loved.* He sent him last of all, saying, 'They will respect my son.'
>
> "But the tenants said to one another, *'This is the heir. Come, let's kill him, and the inheritance will be ours.' So they took him and killed him,* and threw him out of the vineyard.
>
> *"What then will the owner of the vineyard do? He will come and kill those tenants and give the vineyard to others.* Haven't you read this scripture:
>
> *'The stone the builders rejected has become the capstone; the Lord has done this, and it is marvellous in our eyes'?"*
>
> *Then they looked for a way to arrest him because they knew he had spoken the parable against them. But they were afraid of the crowd; so they left him and went away.*
>
> (12:1–12)

Some useful clues to unlock the meaning of this parable

- Vineyard owner who lives far away = God.

- The vineyard = the Jewish nation.

- Owner's servants = prophets who have brought God's message to people in the past.

- Owner's son = Jesus.

- Tenants who abuse and kill the servants = Jewish leaders.

Activity 1

Using these clues, rewrite the parable of the tenants to reveal its true meaning.

What does this parable show about the costs of discipleship for Christians today?

Once decoded, it is clear that the parable is prophesying Jesus' crucifixion. However, it also tells Christians what the price of discipleship may mean for them. Like Jesus, they too may be called to face abuse, torture and even death for their beliefs. Many Christians today would think that this is a high price to pay and some would question whether their death would be worth it. The parable ends with the promise that God will recognize their sacrifice.

Activity 2

Research the life and death of Oscar Romero. In pairs, decide how you could liken his life to the rejected stone and his legacy to the capstone.

The stones that crown the top of this wall are the capstones. They were rejected by the builders because they were not the right shape for the main body of the wall.

Archbishop Oscar Romero knew the risks he ran by speaking out against atrocities in San Salvador, but as a Christian he believed it was his duty. Openly criticizing the corruption of the government and preaching Jesus' message of love led to Romero being assassinated. Do you think it was a price worth paying?

✓ Check you have learnt:

- what the parable of the tenants means
- which parts foretell Jesus' death
- what the parable means for Christians today.

TRY YOUR SKILL AT THIS

The (c) question:

Explain why the parable of the tenants might be difficult for modern Christians to accept. (8)

DO YOU KNOW?

The (a) question

Check your knowledge of these five **KEYWORDS** you have learnt:

self-sacrifice
(page 18)

the commandments
(page 20)

the eye of a needle
(page 20)

true family
(page 16)

true greatness
(page 18)

> ✳ **TRY THIS** ✳
> Practise writing out the meaning of each keyword exactly as it is given in this textbook. Learn it, so you can recite it to a partner.

Now mark your answer according to the mark scheme below. This is how the examiner will be looking to reward your (a) answer. Any wording is acceptable as long as you get the right meaning.

Partially correct answer.	1 mark
Correct answer.	2 marks

The (c) question

This question carries the most marks on the paper – **8 marks**.

Here is a typical question you might expect to see on the exam paper:

> **Explain why Jesus' idea of true greatness can cause problems for some Christians today.** (8)

This is how the examiner will be looking to reward your (c) answer:

> In Section 1, there will be an extra 4 marks awarded across all questions for accurate spelling, punctuation and grammar.

Level 1	● One brief reason. ● Not explaining but describing the issue.	1–2 marks
Level 2	● Two brief reasons. ● One expanded reason.	3–4 marks
Level 3	● Three brief reasons. ● One fully developed reason. ● Two reasons with one expanded.	5–6 marks
Level 4	● Four brief reasons. ● Two expanded reasons. ● Three reasons with one expanded.	7–8 marks

Try your skill at answering the (c) question above. When you have checked it through, look at the marking grid and decide what level you have achieved. The examiner will also be looking at your **Q**uality of **W**ritten **C**ommunication in this question, so be sure to write in full sentences, checking your spelling and grammar.

A tip:

The (c) question tests your understanding of the material. It does not ask for your views, so read through your answer to check how you have answered it.

WHAT DO YOU THINK?

The (b) question

Here is a typical (b) question that asks for your opinion and **two** reasons to support it.

> Do you think Christians have to be poor?
> Give **two** reasons for your point of view.   (4)

This is how the examiner will be looking to reward your (b) answer:

● Your opinion + brief reason.	1 mark
● Your opinion + two brief reasons. ● Your opinion + one expanded reason.	2 marks
● Your opinion + one brief and one expanded reason.	3 marks
● Your opinion + two expanded reasons.	4 marks

Try your skill at the (b) question above. Concentrate on giving **two** reasons. Then look at the marking grid to see how well you did.

The (d) question

Here, you are asked what you think about something and then what people who disagree with you think. A typical sort of question you might see would be:

> 'Christians must be prepared to give their life for their beliefs.'
>
> In your answer you should refer to Christianity.
> (i) Do you agree? Give reasons for your opinion.   (3)
> (ii) Give reasons why some people may disagree with you.   (3)

This is how the examiner will be looking to reward your (d) answer for both parts (i) and (ii):

● One brief reason.	1 mark
● Two brief reasons. ● One expanded reason.	2 marks
● Two expanded reasons. ● One well explained reason.	3 marks

This grid shows you that it's worth giving at least **two** reasons to support your view, and the more you can explain them the better.

Remember: Because this is a Religious Studies paper, you have to include what Christians think about the issue. It may be that you share the same view and so it would be covered in part (i), or you may disagree with their views and put their opinion in part (ii); either way you must tell the examiner that *'A Christian would say...'* or *'A Christian would agree/disagree with me because...'*

The mark scheme states that candidates who do not refer to Christianity in either part (i) or (ii) cannot go beyond 3 marks for the whole of the (d) question. This would seriously reduce your marks!

1.7 Jesus casts the spirit out of a boy

In this topic you will examine how the problems of discipleship are shown in the spirit cast out of a boy and why this teaching causes problems for some Christians today.

The background

Jesus had just come down from the mountain where Peter, James and John had seen him appear in glory alongside Elijah and Moses (the transfiguration, which you will study on pages 104–105).

> When they came to the other disciples, they saw a large crowd around them and the teachers of the law arguing with them. As soon as all the people saw Jesus, they were overwhelmed with wonder and ran to greet him.
>
> "What are you arguing with them about?" he asked.
>
> A man in the crowd answered, "Teacher, *I brought you my son, who is possessed by a spirit that has robbed him of speech. Whenever it seizes him, it throws him to the ground. He foams at the mouth, gnashes his teeth and becomes rigid. I asked your disciples to drive out the spirit, but they could not."*
>
> *"O unbelieving generation," Jesus replied, "how long shall I stay with you? How long shall I put up with you?* Bring the boy to me."
>
> So they brought him. When the spirit saw Jesus, it immediately threw the boy into a convulsion. He fell to the ground and rolled around, foaming at the mouth.
>
> Jesus asked the boy's father, "How long has he been like this?"
>
> "From childhood," he answered. "It has often thrown him into fire or water to kill him. But if you can do anything, take pity on us and help us."
>
> *"'If you can'?" said Jesus. "Everything is possible for him who believes."*
>
> Immediately the boy's father exclaimed, *"I do believe; help me overcome my unbelief!"*
>
> When Jesus saw that a crowd was running to the scene, he rebuked the evil spirit. "You deaf and mute spirit," he said, *"I command you, come out of him and never enter him again."*
>
> The spirit shrieked, convulsed him violently and came out. The boy looked so much like a corpse that many said, "He's dead." But Jesus took him by the hand and lifted him to his feet, and he stood up.
>
> After Jesus had gone indoors, his disciples asked him privately, "Why couldn't we drive it out?"
>
> He replied, *"This kind can come out only by prayer."*
>
> (9:14–29)

The symptoms match those of an epileptic fit. People at the time thought illnesses were caused by evil powers.

The disciples failed despite Jesus giving them power to cast out evil spirits (see page 12).

Jesus showed exasperation with the crowd for not having faith in the power of healing.

Jesus pinpointed that faith was at the heart of this problem. The disciples doubted they could do it and when the father said "If you can" it showed he, too, had doubts.

The father's belief in Jesus and faith in his powers caused Jesus to banish the evil spirit from his son.

Jesus had authority over evil. He commanded and the evil spirit was forced to obey.

The central point of the story: only by trusting in the power of prayer can evil be overcome.

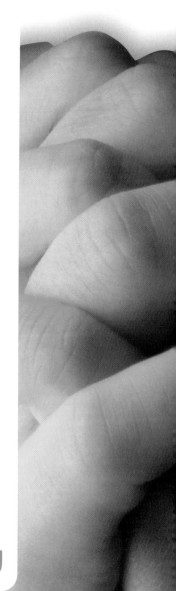

This artist has shown a 'before' and 'after' scene in the same painting. The boy who was thrashing around in a world of grey in his illness now stands fully recovered alongside Jesus and bathed in golden light. Who do you think are gesticulating around the boy on the right-hand side of the painting?

What is the importance of this teaching?

This story is one of several in which Jesus displayed his God-given power to heal people, but this account is teaching far more than that. It is important because the disciples failed to heal the child even though Jesus had given them authority over evil spirits (see page 12). The disciples didn't really trust that they had received that sort of power from Jesus.

When faced with such a difficult task like this, Jesus told the disciples that they should have faith in God to help them and to pray to him for strength to tackle the job.

Why does this teaching cause problems for Christians today?

For some Christians, stories about casting out evil spirits have no relevance today. The medical symptoms in this story suggest the boy was suffering from epilepsy, which has no connection with supernatural forces; it requires modern drugs to control it.

This leads some Christians to argue that Jesus did not heal the boy at all, but just happened to be present at the moment when the boy recovered from his fit. There is no evidence to show what happened after Jesus and the crowds had left. The boy might well have continued to experience similar attacks in the future.

Other Christians find problems because even the disciples, Jesus' hand-picked followers, were unable to do anything. What chance do modern Christians, who have never met Jesus in the flesh, have of succeeding?

If the story is about faith, then modern Christians can learn from it. When people have no faith in their abilities and give up, then failure is certain. Those who trust and pray are far more likely to succeed.

Explain the connection between prayer and the story of Jesus casting the spirit out of a boy.

Activity 1

Some people say this story is more about the lessons the disciples had to learn than it is about the power of Jesus. What evidence could support this view? Do you agree?

Activity 2

a) In pairs, find evidence to support the idea that Mark's story is about faith: the crowd's faith, the disciples' faith and the father's faith.

b) Display your findings as a spider diagram with the title FAITH in the centre.

 Check you have learnt:

- what happens in the story of the spirit cast out of a boy
- why the disciples failed
- what the story teaches about faith and prayer
- two problems Christians today may have with this story.

TRY YOUR SKILL AT THIS

The (d) question:

'Stories about demons have no relevance for Christians today.'

In your answer you should refer to Christianity.

(i) Do you agree? Give reasons for your opinion. (3)

(ii) Give reasons why some people may disagree with you. (3)

The parable of the sower

In this topic you will study how the problems of discipleship are shown in the parable of the sower and why Mark's account causes problems for some Christians today.

the kingdom the rule of God in people's lives

The background

Jesus told this parable at a time when his followers were struggling with persecution and the distractions of everyday life. The story was designed to encourage them to stay loyal and focused on their mission.

Jesus used parables in order to teach the crowds about God.

Jesus said that God's kingdom was only for the Twelve he had chosen. His teachings were in parables to ensure the crowds didn't understand and didn't repent and get saved.

Jesus taught that those who accept God's word and act on it will be very successful.

> Again Jesus began to teach by the lake. The crowd that gathered around him was so large that he got into a boat and sat in it out on the lake, while all the people were along the shore at the water's edge. *He taught them many things by parables*, and in his teaching said: "Listen! A farmer went out to sow his seed. As he was scattering the seed, some fell along the path, and the birds came and ate it up. Some fell on rocky places, where it did not have much soil. It sprang up quickly, because the soil was shallow. But when the sun came up, the plants were scorched, and they withered because they had no root. Other seed fell among thorns, which grew up and choked the plants, so that they did not bear grain. Still other seed fell on good soil. It came up, grew and produced a crop, multiplying thirty, sixty, or even a hundred times."
>
> Then Jesus said, "He who has ears to hear, let him hear."
>
> When he was alone, the Twelve and the others around him asked him about the parables. He told them, *"The secret of the kingdom of God has been given to you. But to those on the outside everything is said in parables so that, 'they may be ever seeing but never perceiving, and ever hearing but never understanding; otherwise they might turn and be forgiven!'"*
>
> Then Jesus said to them, "Don't you understand this parable? How then will you understand any parable? The farmer sows the word. Some people are like seed along the path, where the word is sown. As soon as they hear it, Satan comes and takes away the word that was sown in them. Others, like seed sown on rocky places, hear the word and at once receive it with joy. But since they have no root, they last only a short time. When trouble or persecution comes because of the word, they quickly fall away. Still others, like seed sown among thorns, hear the word; but the worries of this life, the deceitfulness of wealth and the desires for other things come in and choke the word, making it unfruitful. *Others, like seed sown on good soil, hear the word, accept it, and produce a crop – thirty, sixty or even a hundred times what was sown."*
>
> (4:1–20)

What is this parable about?

In this parable, Jesus told his followers about the way different people react to God's message. Only some of those who hear it will actually understand and act on the message. They will be the ones who are rewarded. **The kingdom** of God is reserved for a select few and not everyone.

This is the key to understanding the parable:

> The seed among thorns = people who hear God's word, but the pressures of everyday life swamp them and nothing is done.

> The seed on good ground = people who hear the teachings and respond. They pass on the teachings so God's message spreads far and wide.

> The seed on rocky places = people who start off very enthusiastic, but get distracted by other things and forget all about it.

> The seed on the path = people who hear the teachings but ignore them.

The seed = the word of God

Activity 1

a) Retell this story as a modern parable. You could set it amongst a group of musicians or a sports team, or you may have a better idea. Don't forget to include the categories of people shown in the spider diagram.

b) Give a modern example of each type of person listed in the spider diagram.

Activity 2

For discussion: What matters most, that Mark's Gospel contains the actual words spoken by Jesus or that the message is helpful to Christians?

Keep a note of some of the different views raised because they can be helpful for exam answers.

✓ **Check you have learnt:**

- what the parable of the sower states
- the four different ways people might react to Jesus' teachings
- three problems Christians today might have with this parable.

TRY YOUR SKILL AT THIS

The (b) question:

Do you think the parable of the sower helps Christians to understand the problems of discipleship?

Give **two** reasons for your point of view. (4)

Why does Mark's account cause problems for Christians today?

Christians often find this one of the most problematic parables. On the face of it, it seems to work like the spider diagram shown above, but further investigation shows ambiguities.

One problem is that Jesus said he used parables to help people to understand things, yet the disciples never understood this one. They had to have a separate lesson about its meaning. If they didn't understand its meaning, what chance do later Christians who have never met Jesus have? Once the meaning is understood, what is a Christian supposed to do to prevent the problem of 'seed' falling in the wrong place?

When Jesus was explaining things to the disciples he said a strange thing about his use of parables. He said that he spoke in parables so the crowd wouldn't understand the message and, consequently, wouldn't be able to repent and be forgiven by God. This seems to contradict most of Jesus' teachings elsewhere, which state that the kingdom of heaven is open to all believers.

All this has led biblical scholars to question whether Mark wrote down exactly what Jesus said. Scholars studying the original gospel in Greek have noticed that only the language in the first part of the story reflects the way Jesus usually spoke. The second part seems to be spoken by someone else. Mark was writing his gospel at a time of great persecution; therefore, some scholars believe that he interpreted it himself to encourage the early Christians not to give up in the face of difficulties. This would fit with the final part of the extract where it states that, although many of the seeds fail to grow, the ones that do grow flourish so well that they more than make up for the failures.

1.9 Jesus and service

In this topic you will study how the problems of discipleship are shown in Jesus and service and what it means for Christians living today.

Useful specialist language

Gentile anyone who is not Jewish

The background

James and John, the Sons of Zebedee, asked Jesus for the privilege of sitting on either side of him in heaven. Jesus asked them whether they were prepared to share his whole life from baptism through to drinking from the same cup. Despite them saying they were, Jesus said only God decides the places in heaven. The arrogance of James and John upset the other ten disciples.

Jesus referred to their rulers – the Romans, who were non-Jews, who controlled a vast empire with highly-trained officials and military power.

Jesus contrasted the pomposity of the Roman soldiers with the lowliness of a slave. His followers must be as humble as the slave.

Jesus emphasized his humanity by using the title 'Son of Man', showing he was closer to the humble servant than the person at the top.

Jesus predicted his death when he spoke of giving his life. He was also saying that the purpose of his death was to pay a ransom. His sacrifice would save the whole of humanity from their sins.

> " When the ten heard about this, they became indignant with James and John. Jesus called them together and said, "You know *that those who are regarded as rulers of the Gentiles lord it over them*, and their high officials exercise authority over them. Not so with you. Instead, *whoever wants to become great among you must be your servant, and whoever wants to be first must be slave of all*. For even *the Son of Man did not come to be served, but to serve*, and *to give his life as a ransom for many*."
>
> (10:41–45) "

Activity 1

Explain how this passage from Mark's Gospel adds to the ideas you studied about true greatness on pages 18–19.

The importance of this passage

Jesus used the tensions that had arisen between the disciples about who was most important to teach his followers that true discipleship means completely the opposite. Once again, Jesus turned traditional ideas about greatness on their head by putting the slave and the servant ahead of their master in God's kingdom. The theme of 'the first being last' and 'the last being first' in the kingdom of heaven appears regularly throughout Mark's Gospel.

Just before this passage, Jesus had told James and John that they must be prepared to drink from Jesus' cup if they wanted to join him in heaven. Jesus was predicting his own suffering and death. He was doing so again in this gospel passage when he told them he would give his life as a ransom for everybody. This means that Jesus' true followers have to be prepared to share in his suffering.

Activity 2

Write an Internet advert for an aid worker's job with a Christian charity. State where you want them to work and what they will be doing. Explain how this job fits in with the idea of Christian service.

Why might some Christians say tasks such as helping the homeless are a greater test of discipleship than preaching the gospel in church? Why might a preacher disagree?

What does this account of service mean for Christians today?

Mark's account teaches Christians that discipleship involves undertaking menial tasks. It is not the high-profile do-gooders who impress God, but the people who quietly show concern for others.

It shows Christians that God will judge his followers using different criteria to the ones the modern world uses to judge people. In God's world, it is the servant, not the master, who is the most important.

Although Jesus was saying that the price of discipleship was high, he was also showing that the rewards in the kingdom of heaven are great for those who follow his path.

Jesus contrasted his leadership with the autocratic power of Roman officials.

Check you have learnt:

- what Jesus said about the Christian idea of greatness
- what Jesus said Christian service involves
- what this means for Christians today.

TRY YOUR SKILL AT THIS

The (c) question:

Explain why Jesus' ideas of service may cause problems for Christians living today. (8)

The failure of the disciples

In this topic you will examine how the problems of discipleship are shown in the failure of the disciples and how it might both help, and cause problems for, Christians today.

The background

Jesus had celebrated the feast of Passover with his disciples. This meal, during which Jesus took bread and wine and shared it with the Twelve, is called the Last Supper. During the meal, Jesus made several disturbing prophecies about his forthcoming death. It was late when the group went out to the Garden of Gethsemane on the Mount of Olives. Not surprisingly, after a confusing and unsettling evening, the disciples were very tired.

> "You will all fall away," Jesus told them, *"for it is written: 'I will strike the shepherd, and the sheep will be scattered.' But after I have risen, I will go ahead of you into Galilee."*
>
> Peter declared, "Even if all fall away, I will not."
>
> "I tell you the truth," Jesus answered, "today – yes, tonight – *before the cock crows twice you yourself will disown me three times."*
>
> *But Peter insisted emphatically, "Even if I have to die with you, I will never disown you." And all the others said the same.*
>
> They went to a place called Gethsemane, and Jesus said to his disciples, "Sit here while I pray." He took Peter, James and John along with him, and he began to be deeply distressed and troubled. "My soul is overwhelmed with sorrow to the point of death," he said to them. *"Stay here and keep watch."*
>
> Going a little farther, he fell to the ground and prayed that if possible the hour might pass from him. "Abba, Father," he said, "everything is possible for you. Take this cup from me. Yet not what I will, but what you will."
>
> Then *he returned to his disciples and found them sleeping. "Simon," he said to Peter, "are you asleep? Could you not keep watch for one hour? Watch and pray so that you will not fall into temptation. The spirit is willing, but the body is weak."*
>
> Once more he went away and prayed the same thing. When he came back, he again found them sleeping, because their eyes were heavy. They did not know what to say to him.
>
> *Returning the third time, he said to them, "Are you still sleeping and resting? Enough! The hour has come. Look, the Son of Man is betrayed into the hands of sinners.* Rise! Let us go! Here comes my betrayer!"
>
> (14:27–42)

Jesus' quotation from the scriptures showed that he already knew how his followers would react at the first sign of trouble.

Jesus predicted his resurrection and told his disciples to find him afterwards.

Jesus already knew that his closest disciple would let him down on three occasions.

Peter was adamant that he would never abandon Jesus even if his life was on the line. The others agreed.

All that Jesus asked of his three closest disciples was that they sit nearby and keep watch while he prayed.

Jesus was sad that his most trusted friends, who gave their word to him, let him down when he needed them.

Jesus showed his understanding of human failings. He knew they wanted to do as they promised, but they were exhausted and could not keep their eyes open.

Three times the disciples let Jesus down. As a result of their failure to keep watch, Jesus' enemies were able to walk straight in to arrest him.

Here, the artist has captured the moment when the disciples could not stay awake any longer, even though Jesus had asked them to.

Lo Spagna, *The Agony in the Garden*, bought 1878, © Copyright The National Gallery 2010

The teachings in Mark's account

This is a story of close friends who promised to stay loyal, but in the end, let down the person who needed them most. It shows just how hard life was for the disciples and for Jesus in the final week of his life, but also the difficulties of discipleship. After the years they had spent with Jesus and the teachings he had given them, the disciples failed. Discipleship requires immense strength of mind and body, which humans struggle with. On first reading, it may seem to be a story of failure.

How could this story help Christians today?

Some Christians take heart from the fact that, although the disciples failed Jesus in the Garden of Gethsemane, they returned after the resurrection and went on to spread Jesus' teachings so effectively that Christianity is a world religion today.

There is also evidence that Jesus already knew about his disciples' weaknesses and forgave them for letting him down. This is because he told them where to find him after the resurrection. The fact that Jesus forgave human weakness is a comfort to many modern Christians who may try and fail.

Others are encouraged to read that even Jesus' closest followers couldn't always attain the high standards of discipleship he demanded. If they failed, then it is no surprise that Christians today can't always reach the mark. It is clear that Jesus knew about human weakness when he said: "The spirit is willing, but the body is weak." He does not condemn his followers for trying and failing.

What problems does this story cause for Christians today?

Not all Christians are inspired by this story because it shows that Jesus demanded the impossible from his disciples. Even Peter, who loved his master well and promised faithfully to keep watch for him, was just too exhausted. If he and the other two couldn't do as Jesus wanted, what chance do modern Christians who have never met Jesus have?

Activity 1

Divide your page into two columns. List the points FOR and AGAINST this being a story that helps Christians today with their discipleship.

Activity 2

Jesus said: "The spirit is willing, but the body is weak."

a) Explain who Jesus was talking to and what he meant by both parts of this sentence.

b) What do you think Jesus' attitude was towards the people he was speaking to?

 Check you have learnt:

- how the disciples let Jesus down
- Jesus' reaction to their failure
- the different ways modern Christians react to this story.

TRY YOUR SKILL AT THIS

The (d) question:

'The story of the disciples' failure is no help to modern Christians.'

In your answer you should refer to Christianity.

(i) Do you agree? Give reasons for your opinion. (3)

(ii) Give reasons why some people may disagree with you. (3)

Peter's denial

In this topic you will consider how the problems of discipleship are shown in Peter's denial and how it might both help and cause problems for Christians today.

The background

After the disciples had failed Jesus by falling asleep, he was arrested. Jesus was taken for trial before the High Priest. Peter watched his master being arrested and taken off, but followed at a distance. When Jesus appeared before the High Priest, Peter was hanging around in the courtyard of the house. It was there that some people recognized him as one of the followers of Jesus.

> While Peter was below in the courtyard, one of the servant girls of the high priest came by. When she saw Peter warming himself, she looked closely at him.
>
> "You also were with that Nazarene, Jesus," she said.
>
> *But he denied it. "I don't know or understand what you're talking about,"* he said, and went out into the entrance.
>
> When the servant girl saw him there, she said again to those standing around, "This fellow is one of them." *Again he denied it.*
>
> After a little while, those standing near said to Peter, "Surely you are one of them, for you are a Galilean."
>
> *He began to call down curses on himself, and he swore to them, "I don't know this man you're talking about."*
>
> Immediately the cock crowed the second time. Then Peter remembered the word Jesus had spoken to him: *"Before the cock crows twice you will disown me three times."*
>
> *And he broke down and wept.*
>
> (14:66–72)

This was the first of three occasions when someone challenged Peter to admit that he knew Jesus.

Peter lied the second time.

Peter's fear showed through when he panicked and began swearing he didn't know Jesus.

With the sound of the cockerel crowing a second time, the full horror of what he had done came home to Peter. He collapsed, distraught that he had let Jesus down, exactly as predicted.

The crowing cockerel is a symbol of dawn. Its crowing also fulfilled Jesus' prophesy that Peter would deny his friendship with him.

What problems does Peter's denial cause?

Once again, Mark's account of events shows how humans continued to let Jesus down. Falling asleep was perhaps understandable because sometimes you cannot fight tiredness. Three refusals to acknowledge Jesus seems much worse because they were a form of betrayal. Peter had been so insistent that he would rather die than deny knowing Jesus, yet every time he was challenged he lied to save his skin. Some Christians might find it hard to acknowledge this man as a saint, with many churches around the world dedicated to him.

If Peter, the disciple closest to Jesus, could let him down again, many Christians wonder what chance they would have of being able to stand up for their beliefs if they were ever really threatened.

How might Peter's denial help Christians today?

Some Christians take heart from the fact that even Peter, Jesus' most trusted disciple, struggled with what was demanded of him. They can understand Peter's response to fear; it doesn't mean everything is lost. Later, Peter did find the strength to carry on Jesus' ministry and he went on to become the first pope.

Although he failed Jesus here, Peter learnt from Jesus' teachings and grew in spiritual strength. Ultimately, he was prepared to die for his belief in Jesus.

When **Peter's denial** is seen in the context of his whole life, Christians understand that he learnt from his mistakes and was still able to do God's work.

Activity 1

a) In pairs, discuss what the likely outcome would have been if Peter had owned up to knowing Jesus immediately.

b) Why might some Christians say it was a good thing Peter did as Jesus predicted?

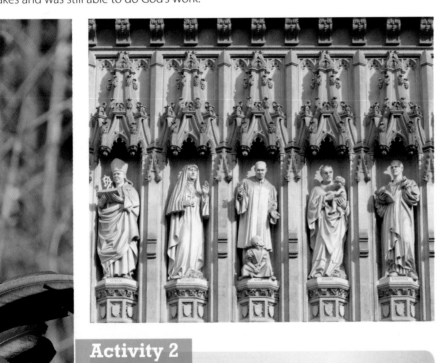

This is part of a series of twentieth-century martyrs whose statues appear in Westminster Abbey. Peter's denial did not signal his failure. He was prepared to give his life for his belief in Jesus and this has inspired modern Christians.

Activity 2

Choose **one** of these twentieth-century Christian martyrs whose statue appears in Westminster Abbey. Find out what situation cost them their life and give a presentation to the class on their martyrdom.

- Maximilian Kolbe
- Manche Masemola
- Janani Luwum
- Grand Duchess
- Elizabeth of Russia
- Martin Luther King
- Oscar Romero
- Dietrich Bonhoeffer
- Esther John
- Lucian Tapiedi
- Wang Zhiming

✓ Check you have learnt:

- how Peter failed Jesus after Jesus' arrest
- what prediction came true in the High Priest's courtyard
- the different ways modern Christians view Peter's denial.

TRY YOUR SKILL AT THIS

The (c) question:

Explain why Peter's denial can be both a help and a problem for Christians today. (8)

SKILLS COACHING 3

END OF CHAPTER 1 CHECK

Check the (a) question

In this chapter about **Discipleship**, you will have learnt the following :

| the commandments | disciples | the eye of a needle | the kingdom |

| Levi | Peter's denial | self-sacrifice | service | Sons of Zebedee |

| true family | true greatness | the Twelve |

a) Choose three keywords from the list and explain what they mean.

b) Which three keywords did you not want to choose? Write down what you think their meanings might be and check them. Or, if you really don't know, look them up in the chapter and write down their meanings. It's better to face the difficult keywords now!

Check the (c) question

Make sure that you understand:

■ the nature of discipleship and why it is important for Christians today

■ the costs of discipleship and why they cause problems for some Christians today

■ the problems of discipleship shown in Mark's Gospel and why they cause problems for some Christians today.

Check the (b) and (d) questions

Check you know different people's responses to the issues above for the (b) and (d) questions.

Remind yourself of two or three reasons the other side gives to argue against you.

Obviously, your responses to the issues above are the most important ones. Rehearse two or three reasons you would give to support your viewpoint on each issue.

Finally, the vitally important thing: how are you going to link it to Mark's Gospel? How could a Christian put that teaching into practice?

Here is a typical example of how questions about *Discipleship* might be presented on the exam paper. Choose one of these questions to work through in exam conditions in order to check your progress.

SECTION 1 – DISCIPLESHIP
You must answer ONE question from this section.

EITHER

1 (a) What is **service**? (2)

(b) Do you think stories of Jesus casting out evil spirits have any relevance for modern Christians?
Give **two** reasons for your point of view. (4)

(c) Explain why Jesus' teaching about true family causes problems for some Christians today. (8)

(d) 'It is impossible to achieve true greatness by keeping in the background.'
In your answer you should refer to Christianity.
(i) Do you agree? Give reasons for your opinion. (3)
(ii) Give reasons why some people may disagree with you. (3)
(Total for Question 1 = 20 + 4 marks)

OR

2 (a) What is **the eye of a needle**? (2)

(b) Do you think the nature of discipleship is impossible for Christians today?
Give **two** reasons for your point of view. (4)

(c) Explain why the story of the boy with an evil spirit causes problems for some Christians today. (8)

(d) 'Stories about the disciples' failures show that today's Christians have little chance of success.'
In your answer you should refer to Christianity.
(i) Do you agree? Give reasons for your opinion. (3)
(ii) Give reasons why some people may disagree with you. (3)
(Total for Question 2 = 20 + 4 marks)

If this had been the real exam, how well would you have done? Use the marking grid to check your progress. Answers to (a) appear on page 9, the grid for (b) is on page 25, the grid for (c) is on page 24 and the grid for (d) is on page 25.

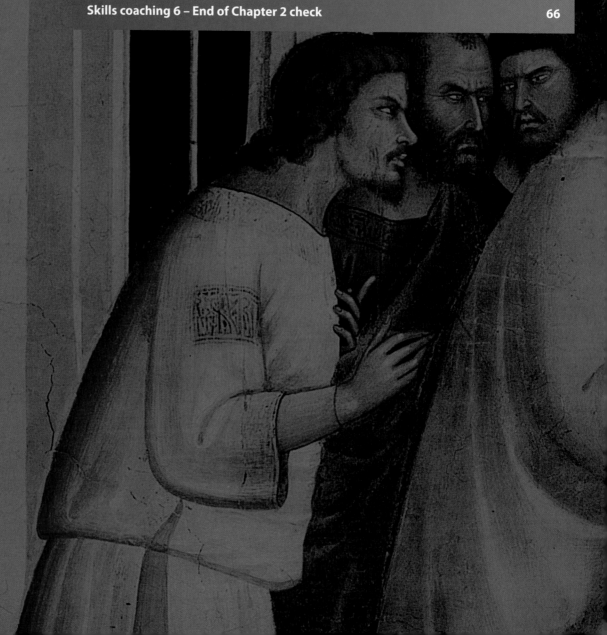

CHAPTER 2

Conflict and argument

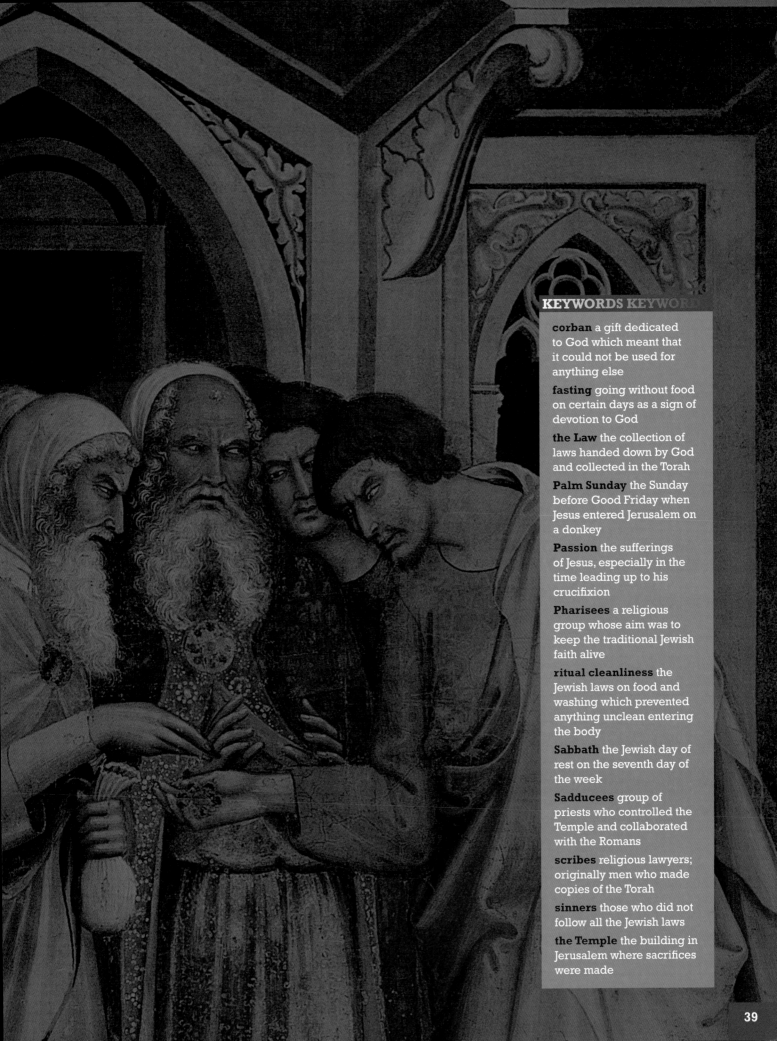

corban a gift dedicated to God which meant that it could not be used for anything else

fasting going without food on certain days as a sign of devotion to God

the Law the collection of laws handed down by God and collected in the Torah

Palm Sunday the Sunday before Good Friday when Jesus entered Jerusalem on a donkey

Passion the sufferings of Jesus, especially in the time leading up to his crucifixion

Pharisees a religious group whose aim was to keep the traditional Jewish faith alive

ritual cleanliness the Jewish laws on food and washing which prevented anything unclean entering the body

Sabbath the Jewish day of rest on the seventh day of the week

Sadducees group of priests who controlled the Temple and collaborated with the Romans

scribes religious lawyers; originally men who made copies of the Torah

sinners those who did not follow all the Jewish laws

the Temple the building in Jerusalem where sacrifices were made

In this topic you will examine why the healing of the paralysed man led to conflict and its significance for Christians today.

KEYWORDS KEYWORD

sinners those who did not follow all the Jewish laws

the Law the collection of laws handed down by God and collected in the Torah

Useful specialist language

blasphemy associating oneself with God/using language or deeds that insult God

absolution God's pardon, granted by a priest, to a person who confesses their sins

The background

This story comes at a time when Jesus had gained a huge following; wherever he went, large crowds gathered. He was famed as a preacher, but some people had heard he could heal the sick. Many people at the time thought that if a person became ill, or suffered from a disease, it was a sign that they were possessed by evil spirits, or they were a **sinner**.

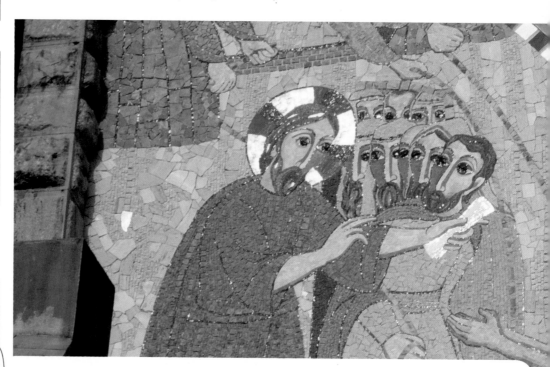

Jesus forgave the paralysed man's sins because the man's friends had faith in Jesus. Jesus said nothing about healing.

Jesus' claim to forgive sins was the biggest challenge to the authorities. They believed he was insulting God, which is blasphemy.

By using the title 'Son of Man', Jesus claimed to be God's representative on earth with God's power to forgive sins.

The healing took place without Jesus needing to do anything else. Proof of the man's healing was shown when he stood up and walked away.

> A few days later, when Jesus again entered Capernaum, the people heard that he had come home. So many gathered that there was no room left, not even outside the door, and he preached the word to them. Some men came, bringing to him a paralytic, carried by four of them. Since they could not get him to Jesus because of the crowd, they made an opening in the roof above Jesus and, after digging through it, lowered the mat the paralysed man was lying on. *When Jesus saw their faith, he said to the paralytic, "Son, your sins are forgiven."*
>
> Now some teachers of the law were sitting there, thinking to themselves, *"Why does this fellow talk like that? He's blaspheming! Who can forgive sins but God alone?"*
>
> Immediately Jesus knew in his spirit that this was what they were thinking in their hearts, and he said to them, "Why are you thinking these things? Which is easier: to say to the paralytic, 'Your sins are forgiven,' or to say, 'Get up, take your mat and walk'? *But that you may know that the Son of Man has authority on earth to forgive sins…"* He said to the paralytic, *"I tell you, get up, take your mat and go home."* He got up, took his mat and walked out in full view of them all. This amazed everyone and they praised God, saying, "We have never seen anything like this!"
>
> (2:1–12)

Why did this cause conflict?

The religious teachers, who heard what Jesus said, had spent years studying **the Law** handed down by Moses and written down in the Torah (the first five books of the Old Testament). From their studies, the teachers believed only God could forgive sinners; no human had the right to claim that sort of power.

If Jesus had simply cured the man, the teachers of the Law would probably not have taken much notice because people with medical skills existed. It was Jesus' claim to be able to forgive sins that caused the conflict. In Judaism, only God has the power to forgive a person's sins in the afterlife. Jesus went on to use the title 'Son of Man', which the teachers believed continued to insult God and the Jewish religion. The title linked Jesus to God and claimed God's authority to forgive sins on earth. This was the most serious religious crime: Jesus was committing blasphemy.

What is the significance of this story for Christians today?

The story reassures Christians today that their sins can be forgiven if they have faith in Jesus. As the Son of God, Jesus had the authority to forgive a person's sins. Christians today believe that what is necessary is faith and confession: a sinner has to admit to their mistakes and ask for God's forgiveness. In the Catholic Church, a priest has been given the power to hear confessions and grant God's forgiveness or absolution.

The story also teaches Christians that faith is an important part of physical as well as spiritual healing. The man in the story was healed because his friends believed Jesus had the power of healing. This might lead some Christians to pray to God for help when they are sick. The Catholic Church has a sacrament of anointing the sick, which grants the sick God's forgiveness.

Some Christians believe that the Church is God's representative on earth. This means a priest can hear a person confess their sins and grant them absolution, which is God's pardon. The priest cannot forgive sins, but Christians believe he has God's authority to forgive the person. Find out the connection between the Catholic sacrament of anointing the sick, and forgiveness.

Activity 1

Write a report that one of the teachers of the Law might send to the Temple authorities about the trouble Jesus was causing.

Activity 2

For discussion: Is it easier in the present day to cure, or to forgive somebody?

Note down the arguments for and against so you can use them in your revision.

✓ Check you have learnt:

- why the story of the healing of the paralysed man is about faith
- why Jesus' words, "your sins are forgiven" were so controversial
- how Christians today understand this story.

TRY YOUR SKILL AT THIS

The (d) question:

'The story of the healing of the paralysed man is not really about healing at all.'

In your answer you should refer to Christianity.

(i) Do you agree? Give reasons for your opinion. (3)

(ii) Give reasons why some people may disagree with you. (3)

Disagreements over the Sabbath

In this topic you will study the disagreements over the Sabbath that led to conflict and consider their significance for Christians today, particularly in relation to current issues of social and community cohesion.

The background

The success of Jesus' preaching and healing began to draw the attention of different groups of Jewish holy men. The **Pharisees**, who interpreted Jewish laws very strictly, were particularly annoyed. Here, they challenged Jesus for breaking the rules about working on the **Sabbath**, the Jewish holy day of rest.

> One Sabbath Jesus was going through the cornfields, and as his disciples walked along, they began to pick some ears of corn. The Pharisees said to him, "Look, *why are they doing what is unlawful on the Sabbath?*"
>
> He answered, *"Have you never read what David did when he and his companions were hungry and in need? In the days of Abiathar the high priest, he entered the house of God and ate the consecrated bread, which is lawful only for priests to eat. And he also gave some to his companions."*
>
> Then he said to them, "*The Sabbath was made for man, not man for the Sabbath.* **So** *the Son of Man is Lord even of the Sabbath.*"
>
> (2:23–28)

> Another time he went into the synagogue, and a man with a shrivelled hand was there. Some of them were looking for a reason to accuse Jesus, so *they watched him closely to see if he would heal him on the Sabbath.* Jesus said to the man with the shrivelled hand, "Stand up in front of everyone."
>
> Then Jesus asked them, *"Which is lawful on the Sabbath: to do good or to do evil, to save life or to kill?"* But they remained silent.
>
> He looked around at them in anger and, deeply distressed at their stubborn hearts, said to the man, "Stretch out your hand." He stretched it out, and his hand was completely restored. *Then the Pharisees went out and began to plot with the Herodians how they might kill Jesus.*
>
> (3:1–6)

People were forbidden to reap corn on the Sabbath according to a Jewish rule at the time. The Pharisees were stretching this rule to its limits here.

Jesus cleverly referred to what David, the greatest Jewish king, permitted. Eating holy bread in the Temple, as the Pharisees knew, was a far worse religious offence than eating a few ears of corn in a field.

Jesus told the Pharisees to get things in proportion. God gave the Jews a day of rest to help them, not to cause a problem for them.

Jesus' final statement was a challenge because, not only did he link himself to God, he also told them that his authority was greater than the Sabbath rules.

Healing somebody who was not in a life or death situation was considered work and was forbidden on the Sabbath.

Jesus issued a challenging question to the Pharisees, who were watching his every move to collect evidence against him. Jesus' question was clever because the correct answer would clear him of guilt. The Pharisees didn't answer.

Mark saw this event as the beginning of the plot to kill Jesus. The religious leaders began to join forces with political supporters of King Herod.

What is the significance of these stories for Christians today?

The Ten Commandments state that people should keep the Sabbath holy, but in the twenty-first century this is difficult. Some Christians understand that Jesus is telling them that his way of life does not depend on following set rules. It is the people who matter and the loving intention behind an action is more important than strictly following the rules.

Other Christians still believe in following the Ten Commandments and setting aside one day a week to focus on worshipping God.

What problem does a 'day of rest' cause for social and community cohesion?

Because the UK is a multicultural and multi-faith society, it could raise a lot of problems if every religious group insisted on having one day a week off school or work in order to worship, especially if it did not coincide with the Christian day.

Other people might argue that if a society has rules, then it is important to keep them. What would happen to the community if everybody claimed the freedom to interpret the rules as they liked?

There was a big outcry in 1994 when the UK law changed to permit shops to open on a Sunday. It wasn't just that it might prevent people going to church, but that it was claimed people would be pressured into working on Sundays and family life would suffer. What are your thoughts on families spending 'quality time' together one day a week?

Disagreements about the Law

In this topic you will examine the disagreements about the meaning of the Law and why these led to conflict, and then examine this in relation to current issues of social and community cohesion.

KEYWORDS KEYWORD

corban a gift dedicated to God which meant that it could not be used for anything else

fasting going without food on certain days as a sign of devotion to God

ritual cleanliness the Jewish laws on food and washing which prevented anything unclean entering the body

The background

The Pharisees watched Jesus' every move: collecting evidence to prove to the religious authorities he was not behaving as a strict Jew should. Jesus, however, challenged the petty religious rituals the Pharisees had created, showing how out of proportion their religion had become. In this account, Jesus pointed out how meaningless some of their traditions were and how they contradicted the commandments.

> The Pharisees and some of the teachers of the law who had come from Jerusalem gathered around Jesus and saw some of his disciples eating food with hands that were 'unclean', that is, unwashed. (The Pharisees and all the Jews do not eat unless they give their hands a ceremonial washing, holding to the tradition of the elders. When they come from the marketplace they do not eat unless they wash. And they observe many other traditions, such as the washing of cups, pitchers and kettles.)
>
> So the Pharisees and teachers of the law asked Jesus, *"Why don't your disciples live according to the tradition of the elders instead of eating their food with 'unclean' hands?"*
>
> He replied, *"Isaiah was right when he prophesied about you hypocrites; as it is written: 'These people honour me with their lips, but their hearts are far from me. They worship me in vain; their teachings are but rules taught by men.' You have let go of the commands of God and are holding on to the traditions of men."*
>
> And he said to them: "You have a fine way of setting aside the commands of God in order to observe your own traditions! For Moses said, 'Honour your father and your mother,' and, 'Anyone who curses his father or mother must be put to death'. *But you say that if a man says to his father or mother: 'Whatever help you might otherwise have received from me is corban' (that is, a gift devoted to God), then you no longer let him do anything for his father or mother.* Thus you nullify the word of God by your tradition that you have handed down. And you do many things like that."
>
> Again Jesus called the crowd to him and said, "Listen to me, everyone, and understand this. Nothing outside a man can make him 'unclean' by going into him. Rather, it is what comes out of a man that makes him 'unclean'."
>
> After he had left the crowd and entered the house, his disciples asked him about this parable. "Are you so dull?" he asked. *"Don't you see that nothing that enters a man from the outside can make him 'unclean'? For it doesn't go into his heart but into his stomach, and then out of his body." (In saying this, Jesus declared all foods 'clean'.)*
>
> He went on: "What comes out of a man is what makes him 'unclean'. *For from within, out of men's hearts, come evil thoughts, sexual immorality, theft, murder, adultery, greed, malice, deceit, lewdness, envy, slander, arrogance and folly. All these evils come from inside and make a man 'unclean'."*
>
> (7:1–23)

Here, they were not talking about basic hygiene but a ritual washing ceremony to symbolize Jewish purification.

Jesus referred to the Book of Isaiah to condemn the Pharisees. He justified the actions of the disciples by saying that what matters is what you really feel inside, not what you say.

Corban was a gift to God, which may have been goods or money. Jesus pointed out that the Pharisees would think somebody very holy if they had given such a large amount of corban in the Temple that they had nothing left to help their parents out. But, in fact, the Ten Commandments states 'honour your parents'.

By saying that all foods are acceptable, Jesus challenged the kosher rules that tell Jews which foods can and can't be eaten for religious reasons.

Jesus explained that it is evil thoughts that come from inside a person that make them unclean, not the food they eat. The thoughts Jesus listed are ones which could cause harm to another person.

What brought Jesus and the Pharisees into conflict?

Jesus was making the point that just doing something for the sake of it is worthless if a person's heart is not in it. This caused conflict with the Pharisees who had developed lots of religious rituals that involved **fasting** on certain days of the week, or washing in a certain way. Jesus challenged the Pharisees' obsession with **ritual cleanliness** before touching food, saying that the religious rules had become out of proportion and, as a consequence, the laws of Moses were being overlooked. Jesus argued that people should focus on the harmful things that come from inside a person rather than petty rules. By disregarding the strict food rules set by the Pharisees, Jesus was striking a blow at the heart of their traditions.

Jesus continued to attack the way the Pharisees paid attention to the rules when he spoke of corban. He did not object to gifts being dedicated to God, but attacked the way some people used corban as an excuse for failing to do what really mattered. Jesus said that someone's duty to care for their parents comes first because the Ten Commandments are far more important than other rules. Once again, Jesus was saying that the Pharisees had failed to understand what really mattered to God.

Judaism has rules about which foods the scriptures permit and forbid. This product label shows that the food is kosher, which means it has been inspected by the Jewish court of rabbis and passed as fit for Jewish consumption.

Useful specialist language

kosher rules Judaism has strict rules about the sort of food that is correct to eat and what is forbidden because it is considered ritually unclean

Activity 1

'I am giving up chocolate for Lent,' Shona said, looking very smug when she announced it to the class. But her best friend knew she never ate chocolate anyway because it brought her out in spots.

Explain the connection between this incident and the story in Mark's Gospel.

Activity 2

Storyboard a situation where someone does the right thing but for the wrong reasons.

 Check you have learnt:

- two ways in which Jesus came into conflict with the Pharisees over their rules
- what is meant by saying it is the evils inside a person that matter more than outside rituals
- what some Christians today may learn from this story.

What is the relevance of this story for social and community cohesion?

This gospel story hinges on the reasons why someone does something. Jesus showed that just keeping rules for the sake of it is worthless. What really matters is showing love and care for others and Jesus was prepared to challenge the rules if necessary. Some Christians today have followed Jesus' lead and have shown that they are prepared to break the law if necessary to care for other members of society as Jesus intended.

For others, the story has relevance for issues of social and community cohesion because Jesus is saying that food and culture between religious and social groups are not important: everyone can get on because what matters most is the person inside.

Activity 3

Use the Internet to find out about how Catholic priest, Father Richard McKay, was prepared to break the law to help Rwandan asylum seeker, Josette Ishimwe. How is this news story relevant to the story from Mark's Gospel?

TRY YOUR SKILL AT THIS

The (b) question:

Do you think that if a law exists, everybody should obey it?

Give **two** reasons for your point of view. (4)

DO YOU KNOW?

Improve your skill with the (a) question

In this chapter so far you have learnt seven KEYWORDS.

| the Law (page 40) | sinners (page 40) | Pharisees (page 42) | Sabbath (page 42) |

| fasting (page 44) | ritual cleanliness (page 44) | corban (page 44) |

The best way to be certain of your 2 marks every time is to learn the exact definition that is given. Can you recite it word for word? Don't worry if you can't manage it, other wording is acceptable so long as it means exactly the same thing.

✳ TRY THIS ✳
Write down the definition of each keyword without checking back. Then look the words up to see if you got them right.

Improve your skill with the (c) question

Here is an example of a typical (c) question:

> Explain why Jesus' healing of the paralysed man led to conflict and why that is significant for Christians today. (8)

STEP 1

Copy the question down on your page and underline the important words. Your version may well look like this:

Explain why Jesus' healing of the paralysed man led to conflict and why that is significant for Christians today.

STEP 2

Draw a line down your page and head the first column 'led to conflict' and the second 'significance today'. Note down as many reasons as you can in each column. Look back in the textbook to help you. Aim to put three reasons in each column.

STEP 3

Write up the notes you have made in full sentences, one sentence for each reason.

Start your first paragraph:
'Jesus' healing of the paralysed man led to conflict because...'
Then begin a new paragraph:
'This is significant for Christians today because...'

Use the mark scheme on page 24 to 'Be the examiner'.

WHAT DO YOU THINK?

Improve your skill with the (b) question

This question asks for your opinion. Here are the sorts of things you could be asked about:

> Do you think Jesus should have stopped his disciples breaking the Sabbath laws?
>
> Do you think the Pharisees were right to complain about Jesus' failure to keep Jewish rules about purity?
>
> Do you think Jesus really cured the paralysed man?
>
> Do you think Sunday should be kept as a special day?
>
> Give **two** reasons for your point of view.   (4)

Choose one of the (b) questions above to work on.

STEP 3

To get the full 4 marks for the (b) question, you need to develop each point into a reasoned sentence. So you could write:

I don't think Sunday should be kept as a special day because not everyone is a Christian and those that are may not want to spend all day in church. ✓ (2 marks)

I think you should be free to go to church if you want to, or to have a job, or to go shopping on Sunday. Nobody has the right to tell you how you should spend your time. ✓ (2 marks)

STEP 2

Now note down two reasons you would give. If your reasons are just brief comments, you will only gain 2 marks. For example, if you chose the question that asks 'Do you think Sunday should be kept as a special day?' you might decide 'no' and jot down that not everyone is religious. ✓ (1 mark)

But that is a bit brief, isn't it?

STEP 1

Decide whether your response is going to be 'Yes' or 'No'. There are no marks for saying this, but it is important to be clear in your own mind what view you are going to take.

✓ Choose a different question to answer. When you have completed it, swap answers with a partner and award marks according to the mark scheme on page 25.

In this topic you will study why Jesus' predictions of his Passion might have led to conflict and their significance for Christians today.

The background

As he walked with his disciples, Jesus asked them who people thought he was. They said people thought he was the person who would go ahead to proclaim the Messiah. Peter said that was wrong because Jesus was the Messiah they were all waiting for. Jesus' later predictions of his **Passion** show that he was trying to prepare the disciples for what was going to happen to him. To do this, Jesus had to show them that their idea of the Messiah as a political leader was totally wrong.

Jesus deliberately chose the title 'Son of Man' to emphasize his humanity and the suffering he was to undergo. This contrasted with the idea of the Messiah as a political leader.

Jesus predicted his suffering, rejection and execution, but also his resurrection.

Peter could not bear this negative talk; it did not fit his idea of a Messiah, so he protested.

Jesus told Peter off harshly for not understanding the real concept of the Messiah.

Jesus repeated the idea of a Messiah who will suffer, yet be resurrected.

After Jesus' reaction to Peter's misunderstanding, none of the disciples dared to open their mouths, even though they didn't know what Jesus was talking about.

Once again, Jesus' followers were uncertain and afraid.

> He then began to teach them that the *Son of Man must suffer many things* and *be rejected by the elders, chief priests and teachers of the law, and that he must be killed and after three days rise again.* He spoke plainly about this, and *Peter took him aside and began to rebuke him.*
>
> But when Jesus turned and looked at his disciples, *he rebuked Peter. "Get behind me, Satan!" he said. "You do not have in mind the things of God, but the things of men."*
>
> **(8:31–33)**

> They left that place and passed through Galilee. Jesus did not want anyone to know where they were, because he was teaching his disciples. He said to them, *"The Son of Man is going to be betrayed into the hands of men. They will kill him, and after three days he will rise."* But they did not understand what he meant and were afraid to ask him about it.
>
> **(9:30–32)**

> They were on their way up to Jerusalem, with Jesus leading the way, and *the disciples were astonished, while those who followed were afraid.* Again he took the Twelve aside and told them what was going to happen to him. "We are going up to Jerusalem," he said, "and *the Son of Man will be betrayed to the chief priests and teachers of the law. They will condemn him to death and will hand him over to the Gentiles, who will mock him and spit on him, flog him and kill him. Three days later he will rise."*
>
> **(10:32–34)**

Jesus warned them for the third time about what was going to happen to him, explaining his suffering in detail, as well as his resurrection.

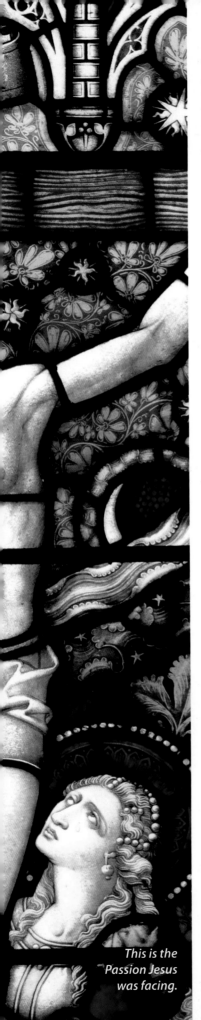

This is the Passion Jesus was facing.

Why might Jesus' predictions have led to conflict?

What Jesus told his disciples was shocking because the person they had devoted all their love and attention to was now predicting his death. That must have seemed like failure to the disciples. Mark shows them reacting outwardly in different ways to Jesus' predictions: Peter spoke up and protested at what Jesus was saying, whilst the others kept quiet. They were all horrified and upset by Jesus' words, but they handled their emotions in different ways. By daring to speak out, Peter came into conflict with Jesus.

This modern depiction of Jesus shows how brave he was in facing his Passion.

What is the significance of Jesus' predictions for Christians today?

Modern Christians hold conflicting views about the Passion predictions. If Jesus knew what was going to happen to him, some have wondered why he did not try to change the outcome. Others have pointed out that Jesus' crucifixion was part of God's plan and so it had to be fulfilled. The fact that Jesus prophesied his Passion three times and used words like "the Son of Man must suffer" makes it clear that his death was necessary.

Because Jesus' predictions proved accurate in every respect, it shows that he must have had some sort of supernatural knowledge. For Christians, the only supernatural power is God. The accuracy of Jesus' predictions supports the Christian belief that he was the Son of God.

Jesus' predictions are also significant to Christians because they bear out passages in the Old Testament that foretell a Messiah who will be a suffering servant rather than a military hero. For Christians, this is further proof that Jesus was the Messiah who was foretold in the scriptures.

Some modern Christian scholars believe that the Passion predictions were never spoken by Jesus but were put in by Mark who, with the benefit of hindsight, wanted to strengthen believers' faith in Jesus as the Messiah.

Activity 1

Draw a flow diagram using the gospel extracts here to show what Jesus told his disciples on each occasion and how he built up the detail.

Activity 2

a) Why did Peter object to Jesus' talk and think it defeatist?

b) What do you think Jesus meant when he told Peter, "You do not have in mind the things of God, but the things of men"?

✓ Check you have learnt:

- the predictions Jesus made about his Passion and resurrection
- why Jesus' predictions led to conflict with the disciples
- the significance these predictions might have for Christians today.

TRY YOUR SKILL AT THIS

The (d) question:

'If Jesus really knew what was going to happen to him, then he would have stopped it.'

In your answer you should refer to Christianity.

(i) Do you agree? Give reasons for your opinion. (3)

(ii) Give reasons why some people may disagree with you. (3)

Jesus' entry into Jerusalem

In this topic you will consider why Jesus' entry into Jerusalem might have caused conflict and its significance for Christians today.

KEYWORDS KEYWORD

Palm Sunday the Sunday before Good Friday when Jesus entered Jerusalem on a donkey

The background

The following event happened at the beginning of the week leading up to Jesus' crucifixion. Everything in this story was triumphant and Jesus was welcomed as a popular hero by the masses when he entered the city. This is in marked contrast to the end of the week when everyone rejected Jesus and he was executed like a criminal.

> Some translations say 'colt', others say 'donkey'. Both indicate a cheap animal that a poor person could afford. Kings or political leaders rode something more impressive, like a stallion or a warhorse. Riding a humble animal showed that this leader came in peace. Mark's account states the animal had not been ridden, which means it had been specially kept for a sacred purpose.

> Jesus was greeted like a hero by the crowd. It was a humble greeting because cloaks were used for a saddle, and cloaks and branches (palms) covered the roadway ahead.

> These words link Jesus with Old Testament prophecies about the Messiah. 'Hosanna' means 'God save us', which is ambiguous. They may have been asking God to save them from the Romans, or from their sins.

> " As they approached Jerusalem and came to Bethphage and Bethany at the Mount of Olives, Jesus sent two of his disciples, saying to them, "Go to the village ahead of you, and just as you enter it, *you will find a colt tied there, which no one has ever ridden*. Untie it and bring it here. If anyone asks you, 'Why are you doing this?' tell him, 'The Lord needs it and will send it back here shortly.'"
>
> They went and found a colt outside in the street, tied at a doorway. As they untied it, some people standing there asked, "What are you doing, untying that colt?" They answered as Jesus had told them to, and the people let them go. *When they brought the colt to Jesus and threw their cloaks over it, he sat on it. Many people spread their cloaks on the road, while others spread branches they had cut in the fields. Those who went ahead and those who followed shouted,*
>
> *"Hosanna!*
>
> *Blessed is he who comes in the name of the Lord!*
>
> *Blessed is the coming kingdom of our father David!*
>
> *Hosanna in the highest!"*
>
> Jesus entered Jerusalem and went to the temple. He looked around at everything, but since it was already late, he went out to Bethany with the Twelve.
>
> **(11:1–11)** "

Why might Jesus' entry into Jerusalem have caused conflict?

The authorities were concerned about anybody who attracted a large crowd in case trouble started. To make matters worse, the crowds seemed to be welcoming Jesus as the Messiah, which for most Jews meant a political leader. Their cries of 'Hosanna' meaning 'God save us' also suggested conflict was on the horizon.

The incident may have also sparked conflict amongst the crowd later when they became dissatisfied with Jesus. The Messiah they welcomed into Jerusalem with shouts of 'God save us' allowed himself to be arrested and put to death without taking any heroic stand against the Romans. They could well have felt tricked by Jesus.

What is the significance of Jesus' predictions for Christians today?

Jesus' entry into Jerusalem is important for present-day Christians because it helps them to understand that Jesus was the Son of Man. His entry into Jerusalem on a humble animal shows them how he identified with ordinary people. The symbolic nature of the entry into Jerusalem is significant because it fulfils prophecies about the Messiah in Psalm 118:25–26 and in the Book of Zechariah (9:9).

For most Christians, Jesus' entry into Jerusalem marks the beginning of Holy Week. It is celebrated in church as **Palm Sunday**, a name that remembers the way the crowds welcomed Jesus by throwing palm branches on the ground.

Some churches re-enact Jesus' entry into Jerusalem on Palm Sunday. Below, the vicar leads the congregation, and a donkey, into church. During the service, it is customary for small crosses of folded palm leaves to be given to the congregation. Why do you think some Christians like to re-enact Jesus' entry into Jerusalem?

Activity 1

File a report from an undercover agent who watched Jesus' entry into Jerusalem. The agent thinks his boss ought to pay special attention as this man appears to be a potential troublemaker. Make sure you add a warning about his popularity.

Activity 2

a) Make a list of the main features in this story.

b) Against each, write its significance for Christians.

Check you have learnt:

- what happened when Jesus entered Jerusalem
- why Jesus' entry might have caused conflict
- what the event means for Christians today.

TRY YOUR SKILL AT THIS

The (c) question:

Explain why Jesus' entry into Jerusalem is significant for Christians today. (8)

In this topic you will consider why Jesus' cleansing of the Temple might have caused conflict and examine its significance for Christians today in relation to current issues of social and community cohesion.

KEYWORDS KEYWORD

the Temple the building in Jerusalem where sacrifices were made

This was the first and only time Jesus reacted violently to a situation.

Jesus knew that the scholars in the Temple would recognize this quotation from Isaiah 56:7 and Jeremiah 7:11. By quoting the scriptures to prove his point, Jesus was threatening their authority. Jesus told them the Temple was for prayer, not trade, and it should be open to everyone; this meant non-Jews.

This harsh condemnation of the Temple authorities infuriated them and made them all the more determined to trap Jesus.

The background

The event described below followed on from Jesus' triumphant entry into Jerusalem and occurred during the final days before his crucifixion. It shows the build-up of tensions between Jesus and the religious authorities in **the Temple** who already felt threatened by his presence in the city. This is the only recorded incident of Jesus reacting violently to a situation.

> On reaching Jerusalem, Jesus entered the temple area and began driving out those who were buying and selling there. *He overturned the tables of the money-changers and the benches of those selling doves, and would not allow anyone to carry merchandise through the temple courts.* And as he taught them, he said, *"Is it not written: 'My house will be called a house of prayer for all nations'? But you have made it 'a den of robbers'."*
>
> *The chief priests and the teachers of the law heard this and began looking for a way to kill him, for they feared him, because the whole crowd was amazed at his teaching.*
>
> (11:15–18)

Activity 1

Explain why the quote: "'My house will be called a house of prayer for all nations'? But you have made it 'a den of robbers'." contains all the important points in this story.

Some Christians believe that the commercialization of their religion is totally wrong. What harm could this sort of trading do in a place of worship? Why might other Christians be in favour of selling religious books and artifacts?

Today, all that is left of the Temple in Jerusalem is this tall section known as the Western Wall. It is a very holy place where many Jews come to pray.

Why might the cleansing of the Temple have caused conflict?

It is very easy to see why this incident might have caused conflict because Jesus reacted violently to the blatant trading that was going on in God's house. The traders would certainly have been furious to have their goods spoiled and their livelihoods disrupted by Jesus' outburst. The Temple authorities would have been incensed by Jesus' actions because he showed them up for permitting trading in the Temple, the holiest site for Jews.

By quoting scriptures to back up his point that the Bible forbids trading in the Temple, Jesus was bound to antagonize the authorities. The scribes and the Pharisees were experts in the scriptures, so Jesus challenged their scholarship when he used such quotations.

Jesus' suggestion that the Temple was "for all nations" challenged the Jewish belief that they were God's chosen race and the Temple was exclusively for Jews. Allowing anyone else into the Temple would have compromised its purity, in their eyes.

What impact does this story have on social and community cohesion?

Jesus' remark that the Temple should be open to people of all nations raises the question of whether all places of worship today should be open to everybody. This idea might not be welcomed by communities who strive to keep themselves apart from the world as part of their religious practice. Some orders of nuns and monks believe that it is important to keep themselves apart from the world in order to worship God.

Groups from minority cultures or religions might prefer to keep themselves apart from others in order to maintain their identity. Opening up their way of life could dilute its unique heritage and possibly ruin it. Equally, some religious groups require ritual purity as part of their practice; this would be lost if just anybody could walk in and out of their holy places.

The issue of mixing religion with shopping is also a contentious issue. By overthrowing the traders, Jesus was making it very clear that prayer and shopping don't mix. This might have an impact on places of worship that are regularly visited by tourists. Some would say that charging for admission and having a gift shop or coffee bar inside a place of worship is exactly what Jesus was objecting to in this story.

DO YOU KNOW?

Improve your skill with the (a) question

Three **KEYWORDS** have appeared in the past section. Using the exact definitions, answer the following:

What is the **Passion**?	(2)
What is **Palm Sunday**?	(2)
What is **the Temple**?	(2)

Using the keywords in your answers will also gain you marks because it shows you can use specialist vocabulary.

> ✳ **TRY THIS** ✳
>
> Here is the meaning of two keywords from Chapter 1. What is the correct keyword?
>
> ? = a metaphor used by Jesus to show that wealth makes it difficult to enter the Kingdom of God
>
> ? = the rule of God in people's lives

Improve your skill with the (c) question

The (c) question is the big one because it is testing quite a few things and that is why it carries 8 marks. The examiner wants you to show that you have a good knowledge and understanding of the topic. This means you *either* need to give plenty of reasons *or* develop the examples you give.

The question is likely to ask you to *Explain why* something is the case. This could be because the account you have been studying has a special significance for Christians or perhaps today's Christians find it difficult to understand, or accept, what is written in Mark's Gospel.

You might find it helpful to think of your answer in terms of a balance:

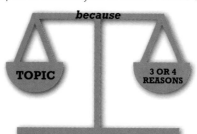

because

TOPIC — 3 OR 4 REASONS

The topic the question is asking about is on one side, for example, Jesus' predictions of his Passion. On the other side are reasons, for example, three or four reasons why this causes problems.

The (c) question is testing whether you know some of the different interpretations Christians have of a particular account in Mark's Gospel:

Explain why Jesus' predictions of his Passion are significant for Christians today.	(8)
Explain why Jesus' entry into Jerusalem is significant for Christians today.	(8)
Explain why Jesus' cleansing of the Temple has relevance for issues of social and community cohesion today.	(8)

Choose **one** of the questions above and plan it step by step as you learnt on page 14.

Question (c) will give **the QWC marks for the exam.**

- So remember to write in paragraphs using full sentences and correct punctuation.
- Check you have included some specialist terms. Are there any keywords you could include?

> **A tip:**
>
> The (c) question is **not** asking for your opinion, so **do not** say
>
> 'I think...'

WHAT DO YOU THINK?

Improve your skill with the (d) question

This is the opportunity for you to have your say and explain your reasons. Question (b) and question (d) are both asking for your opinion.

You practised question (b) on page 47, so let's tackle question (d). It is similar to (b) but also tests whether you can understand someone else's point of view that is different from your own. There are 6 marks for the whole answer, with 3 given for each half of the question.

Here are some typically controversial statements you might see in a (d) question:

'The cleansing of the Temple was unnecessarily violent.'

'If Jesus could predict the Passion, he should have stopped it.'

'The entry into Jerusalem showed that people recognized Jesus as the Messiah.'

The (d) question will then go on to ask:

In your answer you should refer to Christianity.

(i) Do you agree? Give reasons for your opinion. (3)

(ii) Give reasons why some people may disagree with you. (3)

STEP 3

Then tackle part (ii) in the same way, only this time you begin with *'Some people may disagree with me because...'* Express the points in your table as fully as possible.

STEP 2

As you did for the (b) question, start with your opinion. This time it will go in part (i). Start with *'I think...'* and then go on to express as fully as you can the reasons you have listed. Look back to the mark scheme on page 25 to remind yourself exactly what the examiner is looking for.

STEP 1

Draw two columns on your page and head one side *'Agree'* and the other side *'Disagree'*. Write two or three reasons in each column. Check that some of them refer to Christianity.

A tip:

! Have you included specialist language or keywords?

Have you included a religious viewpoint?

Whose authority?

In this topic you will consider why the argument about authority might have led to conflict and its significance for Christians today.

KEYWORDS KEYWORDS

scribes religious lawyers; originally men who made copies of the Torah

The chief priests, **scribes** (or teachers of the law) and elders made up the Sanhedrin, the group with authority in the Temple.

The key to this story hinges on this question.

Jesus' reply was clever. By asking them a question, he avoided saying anything that would play into their hands.

The Temple authorities did not believe that John was a prophet, but the ordinary people did and understood that he came ahead of the Messiah.

Useful specialist language

Sanhedrin the supreme Jewish council in the Temple, which included the High Priest (a Sadducee)

Activity 1

Here is a trick question because, no matter whether you answer 'Yes' or 'No', you are left feeling guilty: 'Have you stopped skiving off school?'

Think of **two** more trick questions.

The background

This story shows the continuing build-up of tension between Jesus and the leaders in the Temple. It follows the cleansing of the Temple when Jesus publicly challenged the authorities and won. From then on, the authorities were looking for ways to trap Jesus into saying something that would condemn him. By using their detailed knowledge of the scriptures, the scribes attempted to catch Jesus out with a trick question: whatever answer he gave would provide them with ammunition to denounce him.

> They arrived again in Jerusalem, and while Jesus was walking in the temple courts, the *chief priests, the teachers of the law and the elders came to him.* "By what authority are you doing these things?" they asked. "And *who gave you authority to do this?*"
>
> Jesus replied, "I will ask you one question. Answer me, and I will tell you by what authority I am doing these things. *John's baptism – was it from heaven, or from men?* Tell me!"
>
> They discussed it among themselves and said, *"If we say, 'From heaven,' he will ask, 'Then why didn't you believe him?' But if we say, 'From men'…"* (They feared the people, for everyone held that John really was a prophet.)
>
> So they answered Jesus, "We don't know."
>
> Jesus said, "Neither will I tell you by what authority I am doing these things." **(11:27–33)**

Who gave John the authority to baptize people?

A HUMAN DID = John was of no religious importance. The problem was that everybody believed John was a prophet sent by God.

GOD DID = Jesus was the Messiah, because John announced that he was sent to proclaim the coming of the Messiah. The Temple leaders did not accept John's teachings and did not believe Jesus was the Messiah.

GOD DID = Blasphemy, because nobody can presume to know the mind of God.

Who gave Jesus authority to cleanse the Temple?

A HUMAN DID = The removal of Jesus' credibility as a leader, because either Jesus had made it up himself or the Romans had given him authority to behave in this way – which everyone knew was a lie.

Why might this question have led to conflict?

The scribes' question led to conflict because whatever answer Jesus gave would make him guilty of some sin. If Jesus had said God gave him authority to act, then that would have been seen as blasphemy by the Temple officials. If Jesus had said it was human authority, then his actions would have been considered illegal because it was known that the Romans hadn't given Jesus special permission for his activities.

Knowing he was in a no-win situation if he answered directly, Jesus cleverly turned the situation around and asked an equally difficult question of them. The answer to that question would answer his question. Being outmanoeuvred by Jesus infuriated the scribes, since they were the experts in religious law. They felt humiliated because they were forced to admit that they couldn't answer Jesus' question. This only increased tensions between Jesus and the leaders in the Temple.

Why are arguments about authority relevant to Christians today?

Sometimes the law of the land conflicts with what a Christian believes their faith tells them to do. Conscientious objectors always face a problem when war breaks out. Read this peacetime case:

THE EXTRAORDINARY CASE OF THE HAWK VERSUS THE DOVES

In the middle of the night on 29 January 1996, four women broke into the British Aerospace factory at Warton in Lancashire. They slipped past security guards, ran across the runway and managed to force open the doors of an aircraft hangar.

Using ordinary hammers, they smashed the electronics system of a new £12 million Hawk jet waiting to be exported to Indonesia.

After two hours, and more than £1.7 million worth of damage to the plane, they wanted to give themselves up. They tried to flag down a passing police car but when that failed they danced around in front of a close-circuit security camera. Only after a phone call to the Press Association did security guards arrive at 5:00am to arrest them.

In court, the women never denied that they had caused damage to the warplane but they did not plead guilty to criminal damage. They said they damaged the plane to prevent a greater crime of genocide.

They successfully argued that all 24 jets destined for Indonesia were intended for use against innocent civilians in that country's offensive against East Timor. Given Indonesia's record of major human rights abuses and the deaths of 200,000 people (a third of East Timor's population), preventing the export of a jet saved innocent lives.

To many people's astonishment, the jury agreed and acquitted the women.

Andrea Needham, a Catholic and one of the women who damaged the Hawk jet, said:

"I believe that above all else in life, we are called to love and to be human. I can therefore not stand aside and allow the Hawks to be delivered without doing all that is in my power to peacefully resist. I believe that to be silent in this situation is to be complicit with injustice. I pray that what we do today in disarming these planes will be a small ray of hope for our sisters and brothers struggling for peace and justice in East Timor."

Activity 2

For discussion: Is it acceptable for people to take the law into their own hands if they believe their religion is telling them to?

Activity 3

Read the article:

a) Whose authority was challenged when the women smashed the jet?

b) What authority do you think Andrea Needham said allowed her to act in this way?

c) If you had been part of the jury, what would your views have been? Explain why.

✓ **Check you have learnt:**

- why the question the priests asked was impossible to answer
- what Jesus asked in return
- a modern-day example of a clash of authority between religion and the law.

TRY YOUR SKILL AT THIS

The (d) question:

'A Christian should always do what they believe God wants, even if it means breaking the law.'

In your answer you should refer to Christianity.

(i) Do you agree? Give reasons for your opinion. (3)

(ii) Give reasons why some people may disagree with you. (3)

In this topic you will consider why Jesus' answer to the question about Caesar and taxes might have led to conflict and its significance for Christians today in relation to issues of social and community cohesion.

The background

This story shows the escalating conflict that was building up between the religious authorities and Jesus, whom they regarded as a dangerous troublemaker. On this occasion, the Pharisees had joined forces with a political group loyal to King Herod. Yet again, a question was asked of Jesus in an effort to trick him into saying something incriminating. Once again, Jesus outwitted them, which only inflamed their anger.

Two different groups were challenging Jesus here. The Pharisees represented the religious authorities and the Herodians were the political authorities of King Herod.

If Jews paid taxes to Caesar, that showed they recognized the emperor as their leader and not God, which was blasphemy. If they didn't pay taxes, they were breaking the law.

Jesus knew perfectly well what their intentions were.

This answer was clever because you could interpret it as you wished.

> Later they sent some of the *Pharisees and Herodians* to Jesus to catch him in his words. They came to him and said, "Teacher, we know you are a man of integrity. You aren't swayed by men, because you pay no attention to who they are; but you teach the way of God in accordance with the truth. *Is it right to pay taxes to Caesar or not? Should we pay or shouldn't we?"*
>
> *But Jesus knew their hypocrisy. "Why are you trying to trap me?"* he asked. "Bring me a denarius and let me look at it." They brought the coin, and he asked them, "Whose portrait is this? And whose inscription?"
>
> "Caesar's," they replied.
>
> Then Jesus said to them, *"Give to Caesar what is Caesar's and to God what is God's."*
>
> And they were amazed at him.
>
> **(12:13–17)**

This Roman coin is a denarius; it has Caesar's head on the front. Because one of the Ten Commandments forbids people to make images of people who might be worshipped, this coin caused problems. The Romans worshipped their emperor as a god, so coins like this could not be used to pay Temple taxes. The money-changers in the outer courtyard of the Temple changed this money so it could be used. (It was their tables that Jesus overthrew in the passage on page 52.)

Why might this argument have led to conflict?

Given the gradual build-up of conflict between Jesus and the Jewish authorities, any further examples of Jesus outwitting their cunning only increased the tension. One of the problems the Pharisees had was that paying taxes to the Romans acknowledged their authority. Because the Romans worshipped their emperor as a god, and had his picture on their coins, the Jews were in danger of getting involved in idol worship, which was blasphemous and against the Ten Commandments.

Clearly, with the Romans as the occupying power, the Jews would be breaking the law if they disobeyed their rulers' command to pay taxes.

Jesus' answer certainly increased the conflict because it was very clever. It showed the religious authorities that he was more than a match for them. His answer told them that it was important for people to obey the law of the land and to obey the laws of God. Problems might arise though if rulers require people to do something that they believe is morally wrong.

What significance does this story have for social and community cohesion today?

Although no one likes paying taxes, they are a necessary part of funding a modern society. Difficulties can arise when the government decides to spend money on something some Christians believe is morally wrong. As seen on page 57, some Christians hold strong views about warfare and are prepared to take action. For a few Christians, their beliefs have led them to refuse to pay taxes that would be used for war or defence projects.

Others interpret Jesus' teaching to mean it is part of their religious duty to obey the law of the land and, whilst they may object to that law, they would campaign for a change in the law rather than disrupt it.

This story in Mark's Gospel may help some Christians who are living in a foreign country make decisions about whether or not they should take part in civic life, or fight to protect their adopted country. This story is telling them that they do have a duty to support the state.

The Peace Tax Seven, whose members objected to part of their taxes being spent on defence projects, drew attention to their case by dressing up and parading this 'rocket' through the streets.

PEACE TAX SEVEN

26 July 2005

As a protest against the Iraq War, seven peace activists withheld part of their income tax payment. When they lost their case in the UK, they went to the European Court of Human Rights. Six of the seven believed the war was wrong for religious reasons and they refused to pay ten per cent of their tax bill because that is the percentage of the UK's budget defence. The Peace Tax Seven wanted their ten per cent to be spent on peace-keeping and conflict resolution, not armaments.

College lecturer, and Christian, Simon Heywood said, "I am paying money in taxes for something that is simply unacceptable."

Activity 1

Draw a diagram, or explain in words, why either answer Jesus gave to the question about taxes would have condemned him.

Activity 2

For discussion: 'People should obey the people they elected or society will fall apart.' Do you agree? Make a note of the opposing arguments for use in revision.

Check you have learnt:

- why the question about taxes was a trick question
- what Jesus said and its meaning
- the significance of the story for Christians today.

TRY YOUR SKILL AT THIS

The (c) question:

Explain why Jesus' disagreements with the Pharisees about authority are significant for current arguments about community and social cohesion. (8)

In this topic you will examine why Jesus' argument with the Sadducees about resurrection might have led to conflict and its significance for Christians today.

KEYWORDS KEYWORDS

Sadducees group of priests who controlled the Temple and collaborated with the Romans

In Deuteronomy 25:5–6, Jews are told that if a man dies leaving a widow without a son, his brother must marry that woman and produce a son.

No woman can have more than one husband because that is adultery and forbidden in the Ten Commandments. The problem is that if life after death exists, all the husbands would be alive and the woman would be an adulteress.

Jesus said that life in heaven is nothing like life on earth so discussions about marriage were meaningless. The woman would be like an angel, not an earthly wife.

The Sadducees did not believe in life after death, or angels, because there was nothing about that in the first five books of the Bible. Jesus told them they were wrong because in the scriptures God uses the present tense when he speaks to Moses, "'I am the God of Abraham, the God of Isaac, and the God of Jacob'". This must mean that all three men are still alive with God in heaven.

The background

There was continual irritation from the various branches of the Temple hierarchy at Jesus' knowledge of the scriptures. They felt it threatened their authority and so no opportunity was lost to try and trip Jesus up with his interpretation of the scriptures. Groups like the **Sadducees** and Pharisees wanted Jesus to say something blasphemous so they could report him to the Temple authorities, or something politically dangerous so they could report him to the Romans. Here, they invented an absurd religious scenario to see if Jesus could be caught out or, at worst, just appear foolish.

> Then the Sadducees, who say there is no resurrection, came to him with a question. *"Teacher,"* they said, *"Moses wrote for us that if a man's brother dies and leaves a wife but no children, the man must marry the widow and have children for his brother.* Now there were seven brothers. The first one married and died without leaving any children. The second one married the widow, but he also died, leaving no child. It was the same with the third. In fact, none of the seven left any children. Last of all, the woman died too. *At the resurrection whose wife will she be, since the seven were married to her?"*
>
> Jesus replied, "Are you not in error because you do not know the Scriptures or the power of God? *When the dead rise, they will neither marry nor be given in marriage; they will be like the angels in heaven.* Now about the dead rising – have you not read in the Book of Moses, in the account of the bush, how God said to him, *'I am the God of Abraham, the God of Isaac, and the God of Jacob'?* He is not the God of the dead, but of the living. You are badly mistaken!"
>
> (12:18–27)

Who were the Sadducees?

The Sadducees were a powerful group of priests in the Sanhedrin, sympathetic to Roman rule. Their religious beliefs were based on their interpretation of the scriptures. Because there is no explicit reference to life after death or to resurrection in the first five books of the Bible, the Sadducees took this as proof that neither exist. Unlike the Pharisees and other Jews, the Sadducees did not believe in the coming of the Messiah, which made them popular with the Romans who did not want any threat to their domination.

Why might Jesus' answer have led to conflict?

The Sadducees' question was a trick one because they took one piece from the scriptures and deliberately developed it to create an absurd situation, knowing that Jesus had preached about the afterlife. Whichever answer Jesus gave would be wrong. If Jesus had said, "Yes, there is an afterlife", then the woman would be an adulteress with seven husbands alive in heaven. If Jesus had said, "No, she isn't an adulteress", then he would have been forced to admit that there is no life after death.

The Sadducees were furious to have been outmanoeuvred by Jesus on a point of scriptural interpretation; after all, they were religious men with superior knowledge. First, Jesus told them that their idea of heaven was wrong and that people would not be living exactly as they do on earth. Secondly, Jesus told them they had misunderstood a passage of scripture that does prove there is life after death.

Jesus' answer would have also annoyed the Pharisees who did believe in life after death, but only at the end of the world. The scripture passage Jesus quoted proved that Abraham, Isaac and Jacob had already been resurrected.

What is the significance of this passage for Christians today?

Christians today take comfort from Jesus' teaching here because he is reassuring them that there is life after death as the scriptures say there is.

Jesus helps modern Christians to understand what heaven will be like when he explains that none of the things we know on earth will be the same in heaven: Christians will not need their earthly bodies in heaven because they will become angels. This could be reassuring for a Christian suffering from pain because they will be free of this suffering in heaven.

Modern Christians also understand that they are free to decide for themselves whether they wish to be buried or cremated after they die because Jesus is saying their earthly body will no longer be needed in heaven.

Jesus' words teach Christians that resurrection follows soon after death: there will be no waiting for the Last Day before a person goes to heaven. Some Christians also understand that the Old Testament passage is saying that everybody will be resurrected, even if they are not Christian.

Images of angels etched in window panes at Coventry Cathedral.

Activity 1

Explain why Jesus' words, "You are badly mistaken!" would have led to conflict between himself and the Sadducees. Try to include some detail about the breakdown of relations between Jesus and the Temple authorities, as well as what happened here.

Activity 2

Write all the possible answers Jesus could have given to the resurrection question. Explain their significance.

Activity 3

In a Christian wedding ceremony, the bride and groom promise to stay together until 'death us do part'. What is the connection between this promise and the story Jesus told here?

✓ **Check you have learnt:**

- the situation the Sadducees made up to test Jesus
- two things Jesus told the Sadducees they had got wrong
- what modern Christians understand from this story.

TRY YOUR SKILL AT THIS

The (b) question:

Do you think Jesus was right to get into conflict with the Temple authorities?

Give **two** reasons for your point of view. (4)

Generosity or extravagance?

In this topic you will consider why the anointing at Bethany might have led to conflict and its significance for Christians today.

Useful specialist language

nard an Indian herb used in the making of a luxury perfume

The background

This event happened only two days before Jesus' death. When Mark recorded the incident he used symbolism to show his readers that Jesus was the Messiah who was about to suffer.

It was customary for someone to greet a guest by putting a little perfume on them on arrival, but never to this extent. Nard came from India and was expensive. Breaking the jar showed she had used it all up.

Those in the house were outraged by such extravagance and pointed out that the money could have been better used to feed the poor.

Jesus defended the woman's generosity and her understanding that he would not always be on earth. He said people could help the poor at any time.

It was customary to put sweet-smelling oils on a body as part of the burial preparations. Women arrived to do this after Jesus' death (see page 92), but were unable to do so as his body was not there. This woman anointed his body before his death.

> While he was in Bethany, reclining at the table in the home of a man known as Simon the Leper, a woman came with *an alabaster jar of very expensive perfume, made of pure nard. She broke the jar and poured the perfume on his head.*
>
> Some of those present were saying indignantly to one another, *"Why this waste of perfume? It could have been sold for more than a year's wages and the money given to the poor."* And they rebuked her harshly.
>
> "Leave her alone," said Jesus. "Why are you bothering her? She has done a beautiful thing to me. *The poor you will always have with you, and you can help them any time you want. But you will not always have me.* She did what she could. *She poured perfume on my body beforehand to prepare for my burial.* I tell you the truth, wherever the gospel is preached throughout the world, what she has done will also be told, in memory of her."
>
> (14:3–9)

Some Christians argue that the money spent on decorating a place of worship as lavishly as this would be better spent feeding the starving in the developing world. What is your view on this?

Why might this incident have led to conflict?

The conflict in this story is different from the others you have studied previously because it was between Jesus' followers. They were horrified at the woman's extravagance at spending more than a year's salary on a perfume that was used up in seconds. It is also likely that Jesus' close followers, who were men, would have found this unknown woman's familiarity with their great religious teacher offensive.

Even today, Christians are likely to hold conflicting views about whether or not it is acceptable to spend a year's salary on a gesture like this when large parts of the world are starving.

> I did it because it was the best thing I could think of to give him. OK, I have blown a year's wages but, hey, I will never again get the chance to show him how much he means to me.

Activity 1

Draw your own speech bubble. Write inside what someone who strongly disagrees with the woman in this story might say.

What is the significance of this story for Christians today?

Because this story comes only a few days before Jesus' death and resurrection, the event has great significance. The anointing of Jesus symbolizes two things: it shows that this woman recognized Jesus as the Messiah, a word that means 'the anointed one' (see page 120); her actions also foreshadow Jesus' death: a body was washed and sprinkled with perfumed oils before it was buried. The haste with which Jesus was taken down from the cross on Good Friday (see page 90) meant the women had no chance to carry out the correct rituals. They returned on Easter Sunday to complete the anointing properly but never got the chance. This woman's actions ensured the ritual was carried out.

Some Christians see this incident as evidence of the importance of women in Jesus' ministry. They use the story to support their view that women should be permitted to be priests or hold high office in the Church. Jesus underlined the importance of this woman's actions when he said the memory of what she did will be told the world over.

The story also has implications for Christians wondering whether or not it is acceptable to spend large sums of money to glorify God in their place of worship when large areas of the world are starving. This incident shows that Jesus judged what was in the woman's heart as the most important thing, pointing out that she could help the poor at any time.

Activity 2

Create a poster or PowerPoint® presentation to show the links between this story and Jesus' suffering and death.

✔ **Check you have learnt:**

- what happened when the woman anointed Jesus
- why people objected to her actions
- why Jesus defended her
- the story's significance for Christians today.

TRY YOUR SKILL AT THIS

The (d) question:

'It can never be right to spend huge sums of money on a church.'

In your answer you should refer to Christianity.

(i) Do you agree? Give reasons for your opinion. (3)

(ii) Give reasons why some people may disagree with you. (3)

Modern Christians can be torn between giving money to help the needy and using it to worship God.

The plot to kill Jesus

In this topic you will study the meaning and significance of the plot to kill Jesus.

The background

There was a continuing build-up of tension between Jesus and the authorities. The story of the woman anointing Jesus comes between the first two passages shown here.

The Temple authorities knew that Jesus was popular with the crowd and so they needed to arrest him quietly before anyone got the chance to cause trouble.

> Now the Passover and the Feast of Unleavened Bread were only two days away, and the chief priests and the teachers of the law were *looking for some sly way to arrest Jesus and kill him. "But not during the Feast,"* they said, *"or the people may riot."*
>
> **(14:1–2)**

Judas was one of Jesus' 12 closest followers, a person Jesus would have expected to be most loyal. This shows Judas' actions were carefully thought out.

> Then *Judas Iscariot*, one of the Twelve, went to the chief priests to betray Jesus to them. They were delighted to hear this and promised to give him money. So he watched for an opportunity to hand him over.
>
> **(14:10–11)**

Jesus already knew what was going to happen to him and who would be the one to betray him.

> When evening came, Jesus arrived with the Twelve. While they were reclining at the table eating, he said, *"I tell you the truth, one of you will betray me – one who is eating with me."*
>
> They were saddened, and one by one they said to him, "Surely not I?"
>
> *"It is one of the Twelve,"* he replied, *"one who dips bread into the bowl with me. The Son of Man will go just as it is written about him.* But woe to that man who betrays the Son of Man! It would be better for him if he had not been born."
>
> **(14:17–21)**

Having a meal together was a sign of friendship and dipping into the same bowl emphasized the closeness of this group.

Jesus told his followers that what was going to happen to him would fulfil the prophecy in the scriptures.

The betrayal

It was bad enough to be betrayed but what made the situation far worse was that it was one of the people whom Jesus trusted more than most. As one of the Twelve, Judas had been close to Jesus throughout his ministry, sharing the problems and discomforts of his life and preaching the word of God. The closeness of the bond between Jesus and the Twelve is emphasized in this story, which takes place as they celebrate the Passover festival together, even sharing food from the same dish.

Why did Judas do it?

Mark's account gives no reason for Judas' actions, but does mention that he received money for his treachery. Matthew's Gospel states that 30 pieces of silver was the price paid for betraying Jesus. This was not a huge sum of money for the time (only enough to buy a slave), therefore, it doesn't seem that money was the motive.

Some Christians think that Judas lost patience with Jesus not turning out to be the Messiah who would overthrow the Romans. Certainly, Jesus was continually trying to get his disciples to understand that the Messiah was a suffering servant and not a warlord. (Pages 120–123 explain more about the different views of the Messiah.) By manoeuvring Jesus into a corner, some Christians wonder whether Judas was hoping to force Jesus into action.

Other Christians notice that Judas went off to find the chief priests immediately after the scene when the woman anointed Jesus with expensive oil. Perhaps this was the final straw for Judas, who did not understand Jesus' mission.

What is the significance of the plot to kill Jesus?

For some Christians, it is significant that although Jesus knew exactly what terrible things were going to happen to him, he accepted them as the will of God. This has inspired Christians who have found themselves in terrible situations to find the strength to cope.

Jesus' understanding of his fate, including precisely which of his disciples would betray him, convinces some Christians that Jesus was the Son of God who accepted that his death was part of God's plan. Jesus also referred to his death as the fulfillment of the scriptures when he said "it is written", which further proves he was the Messiah.

Others have noticed that when Jesus announced at the table that one of them would betray him, none of them was absolutely sure of their own loyalty, asking "Surely not I?" This gives wavering Christians heart to know that even those closest to Jesus had doubts, yet overcame them. It is also significant that none of the disciples suspected Judas of treachery.

In Matthew's Gospel, it states that Judas betrayed Jesus to the Jewish authorities for 30 pieces of silver.

Activity 1

Draw a flow diagram showing the build-up of conflict against Jesus that culminates in Judas' betrayal. You will need to look back through all of the topics you have studied in Chapter 2 to trace the development of conflict.

Activity 2

Write a memo from one of the Sanhedrin to the High Priest explaining why it is essential that Jesus is killed.

 Check you have learnt:

- the role Judas played in Jesus' arrest
- Jesus' reaction to the plot
- the significance of the plot.

TRY YOUR SKILL AT THIS

The (c) question:

Explain why the plot to kill Jesus is significant. (8)

✓ **Check the (a) question**

In this chapter about *Conflict and argument* you learnt these **KEYWORDS**:

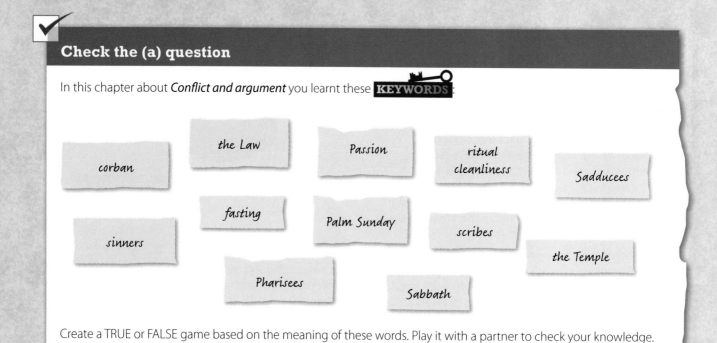

corban

the Law

Passion

ritual cleanliness

Sadducees

fasting

Palm Sunday

scribes

sinners

the Temple

Pharisees

Sabbath

Create a TRUE or FALSE game based on the meaning of these words. Play it with a partner to check your knowledge.

✓ **Check the (c) question**

Make sure that you:

- understand how Jesus found himself in conflict with the Temple authorities
- understand the implications for social and community cohesion in the stories of disagreements about the Sabbath, the meaning of the Law, the cleansing of the Temple, and paying taxes to Caesar
- understand how the ordinary people reacted to Jesus when he entered Jerusalem
- can trace how the plot to kill Jesus builds up.

✓ **Check the (b) and (d) questions**

Check you know different people's responses to the issues above for the (b) and (d) questions.

Obviously, your responses to the issues above are the most important ones. Rehearse two or three reasons you would give to support your viewpoint on each issue.

Remind yourself of two or three reasons the other side gives to argue against you.

Finally, the vitally important thing: how are you going to link it to Mark's Gospel? How could a Christian put that teaching into practice?

Here is a typical example of how questions about *Conflict and argument* might be presented on the exam paper. Choose one of these questions to work through in exam conditions in order to check your progress.

SECTION 2 – CONFLICT AND ARGUMENT
You must answer ONE question from this section.

EITHER

3 (a) What is **ritual cleanliness**? (2)

(b) Do you think Jesus really cured the paralysed man?
Give **two** reasons for your point of view. (4)

(c) Explain why the disagreements about the meaning of the Law
causes problems for some Christians today. (8)

(d) 'Spending money on beautifying the house of God is money well spent.'
In your answer you should refer to Christianity.
(i) Do you agree? Give reasons for your opinion. (3)
(ii) Give reasons why some people may disagree with you. (3)
(Total for Question 3 = 20 marks)

OR

4 (a) Who were the **Pharisees**? (2)

(b) Do you think the woman who anointed Jesus was wasting her money?
Give **two** reasons for your point of view. (4)

(c) Explain why Jesus' predictions of his Passion are significant for
Christians today. (8)

(d) 'If rules exist then people should obey them.'
In your answer you should refer to Christianity.
(i) Do you agree? Give reasons for your opinion. (3)
(ii) Give reasons why some people may disagree with you. (3)
(Total for Question 4 = 20 marks)

✔

If this had been the real exam, how well would you have done? Use the marking grid to check your progress. Answers to (a) appear on page 39, the grid for (b) is on page 25, the grid for (c) is on page 24 and the grid for (d) is on page 25.

CHAPTER 3   Death and resurrection

3.1 The Last Supper

In this topic you will consider the meaning and significance of the Last Supper for Mark.

The background

The festival of **Passover** is the most important Jewish festival. All Jews join with family or friends to celebrate the time when God led the Jews out of slavery in Egypt. Many Jews went to Jerusalem to celebrate the Passover. Jesus was in Jerusalem with his disciples for the **Feast of Unleavened Bread**, which is the meal that starts the seven days of Passover. It took place on the Thursday, and Jesus was put to death the next day.

> On the first day of the Feast of Unleavened Bread, *when it was customary to sacrifice the Passover lamb,* Jesus' disciples asked him, "Where do you want us to go and make preparations for you to eat the Passover?"
>
> So he sent two of his disciples, telling them, "Go into the city, and a man carrying a jar of water will meet you. Follow him. Say to the owner of the house he enters, 'The Teacher asks: Where is my guest room, where I may eat the Passover with my disciples?' He will show you a large **upper room**, furnished and ready. Make preparations for us there."
>
> The disciples left, went into the city and found things just as Jesus had told them. So they prepared the Passover.
>
> When evening came, Jesus arrived with the Twelve. While they were reclining at the table eating, he said, "I tell you the truth, one of you will betray me – one who is eating with me."
>
> They were saddened, and one by one they said to him, "Surely not I?"
>
> "It is one of the Twelve," he replied, "one who dips bread into the bowl with me. *The Son of Man will go just as it is written about him.* But woe to that man who betrays the Son of Man! It would be better for him if he had not been born."
>
> While they were eating, *Jesus took bread, gave thanks and broke it, and gave it to his disciples, saying, "Take it; this is my body."*
>
> Then he took the cup, gave thanks and offered it to them, and they all drank from it.
>
> *"This is my blood of the covenant, which is poured out for many," he said to them. "I tell you the truth, I will not drink again of the fruit of the vine until that day when I drink it anew in the kingdom of God."*
>
> When they had sung a hymn, they went out to the Mount of Olives.
>
> *"You will all fall away," Jesus told them, "for it is written: 'I will strike the shepherd, and the sheep will be scattered.' But after I have risen, I will go ahead of you into Galilee."*
>
> Peter declared, "Even if all fall away, I will not."
>
> "I tell you the truth," Jesus answered, "today – yes, tonight – *before the cock crows twice you yourself will disown me three times."*
>
> But Peter insisted emphatically, "Even if I have to die with you, I will never disown you." And all the others said the same.
>
> (14:12–31)

At Passover time, lambs were sacrificed in the Temple to remind Jews of the lambs sacrificed at the first Passover. Their blood was painted on the doorposts of Jewish houses so the Angel of Death would pass over them. Their deaths saved Jewish lives.

Jesus told his disciples he was fulfilling the prophecy in the scriptures – to show them he was the Messiah.

Unleavened bread was shared at Passover, but Jesus gave the breaking of the bread a new meaning by likening it to his body being broken.

Sharing wine was also an important part of Passover celebrations, but Jesus gave it a new meaning as the blood he would shed for humanity.

By quoting from the scriptures, Jesus explained to the disciples that this moment had been predicted since ancient times; he knew they would all abandon him.

Jesus predicted his resurrection and told the disciples where they would find him.

Jesus repeated what he had told Peter before, that on three occasions Peter would refuse to be associated with Jesus.

What was the meaning of the Last Supper for Mark?

For Jesus, this was the final meal he took with his 12 closest followers before his trial and crucifixion. As the Son of God, Jesus knew this was his last meal and so his words and actions had special significance, even though the disciples did not understand this at the time.

Mark's account of the **Last Supper** links it closely with the Passover celebration. This is because he wanted his readers to understand that Jesus' death signalled the new covenant, or relationship, with God.

Mark's passage shows Jesus as an observant Jew who followed the correct rules for Passover preparation. Jesus had already arranged for a room to be prepared for the meal, which the account describes as an upper room. For the Feast of Unleavened Bread, those preparations would include cleaning and checking the room to make sure all traces of yeast had been removed, as the scriptures required.

Jesus sent his disciples out to collect the ritual items for the Passover meal. These would have included symbolic items like red wine, unleavened bread and bitter herbs.

What was the significance of the Last Supper for Mark?

Mark's account of the Last Supper reminds Christians of the suffering that was to come.

The passage begins by mentioning that Passover was the time when lambs were sacrificed in the Temple, which meant the outer courtyards of the Temple ran with blood from this ritual. The sacrifice of lambs symbolized the covenant, or promise, God had made with the Jews to save them. Jesus was about to shed his blood as a sign of a new covenant between God and his people, which would save them from sin and death.

When Mark was writing, many of Jesus' followers were being persecuted for their beliefs. By emphasizing the connection between the Last Supper and Passover, Mark was giving heart to those early Christians by showing them that Jesus would save those who believed in him.

By making reference to scripture passages, Mark's readers understood that Jesus was the one predicted in the Old Testament – the Messiah they had been waiting for, and the one who rose from the dead to save them.

Wine on the Passover table celebrates God saving the Jews from slavery in Egypt. Jesus gave the red wine a new meaning: that the sacrifice of his blood would save people from death.

The bread on a Passover table is a flat sort of bread made without yeast. It reminds Jews of how their ancestors left Egypt in such a hurry they had no time to wait for bread to rise.

Jesus is often called the Paschal (meaning Passover) lamb. This image reminds Christians of the sacrifice Jesus made to save others. The flag symbolizes his victory over death.

Activity 1

Using words or a diagram, explain how Mark's account links the Last Supper to Passover.

Activity 2

Explain how this passage uses the Last Supper to build up the picture of Judas' treachery.

✓ **Check you have learnt:**

- what Jesus said during the Last Supper
- the links Mark's account makes between the Passover meal and the Last Supper
- what this means for Christians today.

TRY YOUR SKILL AT THIS

The (c) question:
Explain why the Last Supper was important to Mark. (8)

Why is the Last Supper important for Christians?

In this topic you will examine the reasons why the Last Supper is important for Christians.

Useful specialist language

Holy Communion the name of this ceremony emphasizes the way it brings the community together

Eucharist means 'thanksgiving' and is the name some Christians use for the ceremony of the bread and wine today

Commemoration taking part in the ceremony of the bread and wine is to remember Jesus' Last Supper

Receptionism the belief that Jesus is spiritually present in the bread and wine that has been blessed by a priest

Transubstantiation the belief that the bread and wine blessed in the Mass mystically become Jesus' body and blood

The background

Parts of Jesus' Last Supper with his disciples are regularly re-enacted in Christian worship today. The ceremony can be given different names, such as the Lord's Supper, Holy Communion, Mass and Eucharist, but for all Christians it is the most sacred part of their worship because it brings them close to Jesus.

The bread

The priest takes bread in the form of wafers, which he blesses, breaks and gives to the congregation. He is copying what Jesus did and fulfilling Jesus' command to "do this in remembrance of me".

Wine on the altar

In the same way that Jesus blessed and shared wine with the Twelve, the priest says a blessing over the wine and passes it to members of the congregation. This fulfils Jesus' command to "do this in remembrance of me". Some churches drink from one goblet, which they pass to each other in the same way Jesus did at the Passover table. Other Christian groups have individual small cups of wine or dip their bread in the goblet of wine, whilst in other churches it is customary for the priest to sip the wine on behalf of the congregation. In some churches the wine may be non-alcoholic grape juice.

The congregation

Members of the congregation go up to the front of the altar to receive the bread and wine from the priest. By doing this, they are joining with each other like the Twelve joined with Jesus to share his Last Supper.

The priest

By re-enacting what Jesus did – breaking the bread and explaining why, then blessing the wine and sharing it – the priest enables the congregation to share in Jesus' last meal.

The altar

The altar represents the table where Jesus ate his Last Supper with the disciples.

Why is this ceremony so important to Christians today?

Because Jesus was about to sacrifice himself to save others from sin and death, his words and actions at the Last Supper are full of meaning for Christians. When they re-enact Jesus' final meal, Christians are reminded of the sacrifice Jesus made for them.

They believe the symbolic meal, during which they take bread and wine into their own bodies, brings them into the presence of the living Jesus. This enables them to draw strength from Jesus to lead the sort of life God requires of them. It also strengthens Christians' belief that they will share in Jesus' resurrection.

Sharing bread and wine with the congregation brings Christians together in 'communion' with each other, giving them strength to support each other in living a Christian life as they draw closer to God.

St Paul's letter to the new Christian community in Corinth (1 Corinthians 11:23–26) told them how important Jesus' words and actions at the Last Supper were. Paul's account states that Jesus commanded his followers to copy his actions and words in the future.

Because Paul's account includes the command to repeat these actions to remember Jesus, the Eucharist became the heart of most Christian communal worship.

Jesus' words also tell Christians that the wine they share is a reminder of the new covenant God has made with his people through Jesus' sacrifice.

> Paul says Jesus '… took bread, and when he had given thanks, he broke it and said, "This is my body, which is for you; do this in remembrance of me".'

> Jesus '… took the cup, saying, "This cup is the new covenant in my blood; do this, whenever you drink it, in remembrance of me".'

At the heart of worship

Most Christians have a ceremony based on the Last Supper. Only Quakers and the Salvation Army do not because they prefer not to use ritual and symbolism in their worship. Those who do hold the ceremony have different understandings of its significance.

Commemoration

Some Protestants and Non-conformists take the bread and wine to fulfil Jesus' command to do it in his memory. The bread and wine are symbols that remind them of Jesus' body and blood. Some call the ceremony the Lord's Supper.

Receptionism

Some Anglicans believe that Jesus is spiritually present in the bread and wine that has been blessed by the priest. They understand this is what Jesus meant when he said, "this is my body" and "This is my blood". By eating the bread and drinking the wine, Christians believe that they become part of Jesus. They are likely to call the ceremony Holy Communion, to emphasize their belief that, by consuming the bread and wine, they are joined with each other and with Jesus in a sacred way. They may call the ceremony the Eucharist, which means 'thanksgiving' and reminds them of the sacrifice Jesus made for them.

Transubstantiation

Some Christians, such as Roman Catholics, believe that the bread and wine actually become Christ's body and blood. This is because when Jesus took the bread he said, "this is my body" and when he took the wine he said, "This is my blood". Although the objects still look the same, these Christians believe that they are mystically transformed; therefore a Christian who consumes them takes Jesus into themselves.

What do the prayers in Gethsemane mean?

In this topic you will study the meaning and significance of the prayers in Gethsemane, and consider the problems they might cause for Christians today.

KEYWORDS KEYWORD

Gethsemane the place where Jesus was arrested

Useful specialist language

the Trinity the belief that God is one in three parts: Father, Jesus and the Holy Spirit

Aware of the pain and suffering to come, Jesus showed signs of fear like any person might.

'Abba' is an affectionate word for father in Aramaic, like the word 'Daddy'. It showed how close Jesus was to God, his father. Jesus began by asking God to prevent what was going to happen. Jesus talked of a 'cup', meaning a cup of suffering. Then Jesus obediently accepted his fate.

Jesus showed his human side by asking his friends to stay awake and keep him company through the difficult time that was coming. At the same time, Jesus understood that it was very late and Peter was tired. It was only natural that, no matter how much Peter cared about Jesus, he probably wouldn't be able to keep his eyes open.

By using the title 'Son of Man', Jesus emphasized his humanity in the face of Judas' arrival to betray him to the Romans.

The background

After sharing the Last Supper, Jesus and his disciples sang the closing Passover hymn. They then left the upper room to go outside the city walls to the Garden of **Gethsemane**, a quiet garden of olive trees. Jesus went there to find peace to pray to God his father to give him strength to endure the ordeal that was coming. This passage shows Jesus reacting in a very human way.

> They went to a place called Gethsemane, and Jesus said to his disciples, "Sit here while I pray." He took Peter, James and John along with him, and *he began to be deeply distressed and troubled. "My soul is overwhelmed with sorrow to the point of death,"* he said to them. "Stay here and keep watch."
>
> Going a little farther, he fell to the ground and prayed that if possible the hour might pass from him. *"Abba, Father," he said, "everything is possible for you. Take this cup from me. Yet not what I will, but what you will."*
>
> Then he returned to his disciples and found them sleeping. "Simon," he said to Peter, "are you asleep? Could you not keep watch for one hour? *Watch and pray so that you will not fall into temptation. The spirit is willing, but the body is weak."*
>
> Once more he went away and prayed the same thing. When he came back, he again found them sleeping, because their eyes were heavy. They did not know what to say to him.
>
> Returning the third time, he said to them, "Are you still sleeping and resting? Enough! The hour has come. *Look, the Son of Man is betrayed into the hands of sinners.* Rise! Let us go! Here comes my betrayer!"
>
> (14:32–42)

What is the meaning of Jesus' prayers?

Jesus' prayers at Gethsemane give Christians a very interesting insight into Jesus as both the Son of Man and Son of God. As the Son of Man, Jesus showed a very human reaction to the horrors that awaited him. Mark's account states that Jesus was very disturbed and upset by what he knew was going to happen to him, something most people would fully understand. Whilst in this scared state, Jesus asked God to stop what was going to happen. It was the human Jesus who asked his closest friends to stay by him during the coming events.

Then a change came over Jesus and he spoke as the Son of God. Here, we can see obedience and acceptance to God's will when Jesus said, "not what I will, but what you will." As the Son of God, Jesus had the super-human ability to predict what was going to happen to him. The Son of God also understood that his human companions were unable to fight their tiredness no matter how much they wanted to stay awake for him. It was the Son of God who also saw Judas, the betrayer, arriving and who did not run away.

Why might these prayers cause Christians problems today?

Some Christians find it difficult to understand Jesus' reactions in the face of his imminent death. If Jesus is part of the Trinity, then he is God. This should mean he had no need to pray to his Father, nor should he have shown fear and anguish about what was going to happen. If Jesus is divine, some Christians find it hard to understand why he behaved like a frightened human at the start of the story.

The fact that Jesus prayed to God asking him to change the course of events might suggest that Jesus had no trust in God's plan for his only Son. Some Christians might struggle with the idea that perhaps Jesus didn't trust that God would resurrect him on the third day.

Peter's behaviour might also cause Christians problems because, despite his assurances of never letting Jesus down (see page 32), Peter failed his friend. He fell asleep at the time when he was needed most. Christians might wonder at the behaviour of the person closest to Jesus; the man who was to become a saint and the first pope. If he failed Jesus, what hope do other Christians have?

Today, the Garden of Gethsemane is a quiet place where many Christians go to pray and feel close to Jesus.

(see page 32)

Activity 1

a) Describe Jesus' relationship with God in this passage.

b) How does Jesus' state of mind change during the course of this passage?

Activity 2

What do Jesus' prayers in Gethsemane show Christians about his state of mind at that moment?

Activity 3

Draw a Venn diagram. Label the left circle SON OF MAN, the right circle SON OF GOD and the overlapping section in the centre JESUS. In the appropriate section, write text from this passage to show the two roles Jesus fulfilled in this account.

Check you have learnt:

- what happened in the Garden of Gethsemane
- what this account shows about Jesus' relationship with God
- why some Christians have difficulties with this story.

TRY YOUR SKILL AT THIS

The (b) question:

Do you think it is helpful for Christians to see Jesus so frightened before his death?

Give **two** reasons for your point of view. (4)

Betrayal!

In this topic you will examine the meaning and significance of the betrayal and arrest of Jesus in Mark's Gospel, and then consider different attitudes to Judas amongst Christians today.

Judas Iscariot the disciple who betrayed Jesus

Those who came to arrest Jesus were sent by the Sanhedrin, the Temple authorities. At this stage, the Romans were not interested in Jesus' activities.

Kissing another man on the cheek was a normal greeting between friends, but here the sign of affection was used to betray a close friend. The sign was needed because it was dark and the guards had to be sure they arrested the correct man.

One of Jesus' followers reacted violently to the arrest.

Jesus pointed out how unnecessary the big show of an armed arrest was when they could have taken him quietly at any time when he was teaching in public.

Again, Jesus showed acceptance of his fate and that it had been prophesied in Jewish scriptures.

Once again, the disciples let Jesus down by running off when he needed them. At the Last Supper Jesus had predicted "you will all fall away". It has been suggested that the young man who ran away naked was in fact Mark, the gospel writer, who actually witnessed this scene.

The background

Immediately after Jesus had finished praying in the Garden of Gethsemane, an armed guard arrived. These were not Roman soldiers, but an armed guard sent by the Sanhedrin, the Temple authorities. They were led by **Judas Iscariot**. The incident took place in the dark, so the guards needed someone to identify Jesus to ensure that they arrested the right man.

As Jesus predicted, he was betrayed by one of his closest followers.

> **Just as he was speaking,** *Judas, one of the Twelve, appeared.* **With him was a crowd armed with swords and clubs,** *sent from the chief priests, the teachers of the law, and the elders.*
>
> **Now** *the betrayer had arranged a signal with them: "The one I kiss is the man*; **arrest him and lead him away under guard." Going at once to Jesus, Judas said, "Rabbi!" and kissed him. The men seized Jesus and arrested him.** *Then one of those standing near drew his sword and struck the servant of the high priest, cutting off his ear.*
>
> *"Am I leading a rebellion," said Jesus, "that you have come out with swords and clubs to capture me? Every day I was with you, teaching in the temple courts, and you did not arrest me. But the Scriptures must be fulfilled." Then everyone deserted him and fled.*
>
> *A young man, wearing nothing but a linen garment, was following Jesus. When they seized him, he fled naked, leaving his garment behind.*
>
> **(14:43–52)**

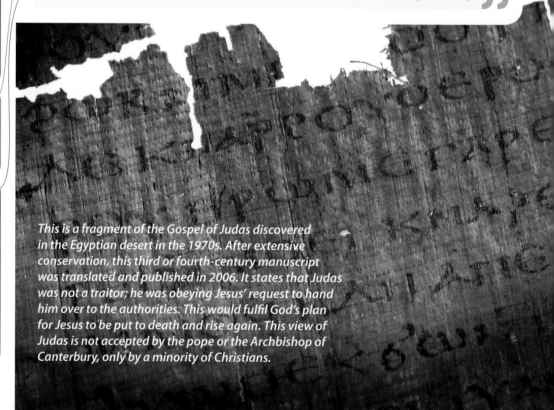

This is a fragment of the Gospel of Judas discovered in the Egyptian desert in the 1970s. After extensive conservation, this third or fourth-century manuscript was translated and published in 2006. It states that Judas was not a traitor; he was obeying Jesus' request to hand him over to the authorities. This would fulfil God's plan for Jesus to be put to death and rise again. This view of Judas is not accepted by the pope or the Archbishop of Canterbury, only by a minority of Christians.

The significance of the betrayal

This event happened in the middle of the night away from public gaze. Jesus made the point that the guards had ample opportunity to arrest him openly, but evidently they were scared his popularity might cause trouble. Any public arrest was likely to provoke a public outcry, which the Jewish authorities wanted to avoid.

The fact that the Temple authorities arrived armed shows that they did not understand the sort of Messiah Jesus was. Jesus had said he was the suffering servant prophesied in the scriptures, not a warlord, although the story shows that one of his disciples was armed because he cut off the ear of the High Priest's servant.

Ugolino di Nerio, *The Betrayal of Christ*, bought 1885, © Copyright The National Gallery 2010

The role of Judas

Judas has gone down in history as the betrayer, just as Jesus predicted: "It would be better for him if he had not been born" (Mark 14:21). His was the ultimate act of treachery because Jesus had chosen him to be one of his 12 closest followers and yet he turned out to be the treacherous one.

Christians down the ages have wondered why Judas chose to carry out this betrayal. One suggestion is that Judas was tempted by money. John's Gospel states that Judas carried the group's money and helped himself to it at times (John 12:6).

Others have thought that Judas was impatient or had become disillusioned with Jesus. After many years of supporting Jesus, Judas wanted action against the Romans. Some think Judas wanted Jesus to show he was the Messiah and use his God-given powers to overthrow the Romans in a spectacular fashion. By forcing Jesus into a corner, perhaps Judas thought he could make it happen.

Some Christians have suggested that Judas was arrested when Jesus cleansed the Temple and struck a deal to betray Jesus in return for his own freedom.

Activity 1

a) Outline the charges against Judas.

b) What might he have said in his defence?

Activity 2

In pairs, list reasons for and against the argument that Judas was evil.

✓ **Check you have learnt:**

- what happened when the guards arrived in the Garden of Gethsemane
- Judas' role in the arrest
- two different attitudes to Judas' behaviour.

TRY YOUR SKILL AT THIS

The (d) question:

'Christians should be grateful to Judas.'

In your answer you should refer to Christianity.

(i) Do you agree? Give reasons for your opinion. (3)

(ii) Give reasons why some people may disagree with you. (3)

SKILLS COACHING 7

DO YOU KNOW?

Improve your skill with the (a) question

Check you know the meaning of the **KEYWORDS** that have appeared in this chapter so far.

| Feast of Unleavened Bread (page 70) | Last Supper (page 70) | Passover (page 70) |

| upper room (page 70) | Gethsemane (page 74) | Judas Iscariot (page 76) |

✳ TRY THIS ✳

Write every keyword and its meaning down on separate cards. Cut out the keyword and its meaning separately. With a partner, lay all the cards with the keywords face upwards on the desk. Lay all the meanings face down in a pile. Take it in turns to draw a card with a meaning from the pile.

You score a point if you can place the meaning on top of the correct keyword. Incorrect meanings go back into the pack, which is then shuffled, to be drawn again.

Improve your skill with the (c) question

The (c) questions in this chapter might ask for the reasons why Christians believe the events surrounding Jesus' death and resurrection are significant today. There are also likely to be questions asking why some Christians today have difficulty understanding accounts of Jesus' prayers in Gethsemane, and his trial.

Remember that these questions will be asking you to show that you understand the different interpretations people today might make from those given by Mark. Don't tell the story of what happened; the examiner is interested in your explanation of the events.

Attitudes towards the disciple Judas are debatable. Not only do you have to consider reasons why some Christians accept Mark's account of Judas' actions at face value, you have also got to know how a few Christians today might understand the man and his actions quite differently.

Here is a typical (c) question you might see about Judas, along with the answer one student has written. It is your job to think about what he has written and how the examiner might mark it.

> **Explain why there are different attitudes towards Judas among Christians today.** (8)

Here is Winston's answer:

> Judas was a really nasty person because he betrayed Jesus and I think that was wrong. Jesus had chosen Judas to be one of his closest followers and that means he shouldn't have turned him in. No Christian would expect their best mate do that sort of thing today. Some people don't blame Judas for what happened. They think he was put up to it but I don't think so. It was terrible what he did.

You are the examiner. Look to see where Winston has shown an understanding of the different attitudes Christians today hold. He also needs to have explained why they think that – look for reasons. Use this grid to mark his answer:

● One brief reason. ● Not explaining but describing the issue.	1–2 marks
● Two brief reasons. ● One expanded reason.	3–4 marks
● Three brief reasons. ● One fully developed reason. ● Two reasons with one expanded.	5–6 marks
● Four brief reasons. ● Two expanded reasons. ● Three reasons with one expanded.	7–8 marks

WHAT DO YOU THINK?

Improve your skill with the (b) question

The (b) question will be asking for you to state your opinions loud and clear! Here are a few questions for you to voice an opinion on:

Do you think the Last Supper matters to Christians today?
Do you think Jesus showed weakness in the Garden of Gethsemane?
Do you think Judas was a victim not a villain?

For each of these questions, write **two** reasons you would respond with.

Daisy has chosen to answer the question, 'Do you think the Last Supper matters to Christians today?'
Read her answer, then look at the marks scheme on page 25 and decide what mark you would give her and why.

> Of course the Last Supper is important to Christians today because they copy it in their
> services and call it Holy Communion. ✓ 2 marks for a brief reason They do this because Jesus
> told them to, that surely must show how much it matters! ✓ 1 mark for another brief reason

The examiner thought this was a good answer because Daisy has given two reasons. One is that Christians have a ceremony based on the Last Supper and she expanded on that by using the specialist term 'Holy Communion' here. Her second reason was that Jesus told them to. If she had expanded on that by mentioning what Jesus told his disciples then she could have got the full 4 marks, but this is a good **3 mark answer**.

Improve your skill with the (d) question

The (d) question is looking for two contrasting arguments, so try these statements:

'The disciples let Jesus down.'
'The Last Supper is the most significant event for Christians today.'
'Judas has been misunderstood by Christians.'

The question goes on to ask:

In your answer you should refer to Christianity.
(i) Do you agree? Give reasons for your opinion.   (3)
(ii) Give reasons why some people may disagree with you.   (3)

This was how Steve answered the first statement above:

> (i) I agree that the disciples let Jesus down. He asked them to stay awake
> and look out for him but they didn't. Mark says they were tired but so
> was Jesus and he managed to keep awake. He had told them several times
> that trouble was looming so they didn't have any excuse.
>
> (ii) On the other hand some Christians would disagree and say that Jesus
> had to die. That was what he had been sent to earth for. No matter what
> the disciples did, the outcome would have been the same. It was God's
> plan. And anyway, the disciples were only human, no wonder they were
> tired. Jesus was the Son of God, he was different. Also, the disciples went
> on and did a lot of good work after Jesus died, so they were not failures.

Use this grid to award marks to parts (i) and (ii) of Steve's answer. Then write a couple of sentences explaining why Steve was given that grade.

• One brief reason.	1 mark
• Two brief reasons. • One expanded reason.	2 marks
• Two expanded reasons. • One well explained reason.	3 marks

The trial before the High Priest

In this topic you will learn about the meaning and significance of the trial before the High Priest in Mark's Gospel, and how it affects Christians' attitudes towards justice.

Sanhedrin the supreme Jewish council which found Jesus guilty of blasphemy

blasphemy associating oneself with God/language or deeds which insult God

High Priest the chief Jewish leader at the time of Jesus

The Sanhedrin didn't have a case against Jesus, yet they had already decided he was guilty and wanted him put to death.

Jesus accepted three titles: 'the Christ', 'the Son of the Blessed One' and the 'Son of Man', which was one of the names God used in the Old Testament, but none of this is blasphemous because he did not use the name of God. For Christians, this confirms Jesus was the Messiah. Some also understand that Jesus was saying he would return to earth again.

When the **High Priest** tore his own clothes it was the sign that **blasphemy** had been spoken and the trial was finished.

Jesus was subjected to physical abuse with people blindfolding him, hitting him, then sarcastically telling him to use his supernatural powers to say who'd hit him. Further torture followed at the hands of the Temple guards.

The background

Immediately after Jesus was arrested he was taken to stand trial, even though it was during the night. The trial took place before the **Sanhedrin**, the supreme Jewish court.

> They took Jesus to the high priest, and all the chief priests, elders and teachers of the law came together. Peter followed him at a distance, right into the courtyard of the high priest. There he sat with the guards and warmed himself at the fire.
>
> *The chief priests and the whole Sanhedrin were looking for evidence against Jesus so that they could put him to death, but they did not find any. Many testified falsely against him, but their statements did not agree.*
>
> Then some stood up and gave this false testimony against him: "We heard him say, 'I will destroy this man-made temple and in three days will build another, not made by man.'" Yet even then their testimony did not agree.
>
> Then the high priest stood up before them and asked Jesus, "Are you not going to answer? What is this testimony that these men are bringing against you?" But Jesus remained silent and gave no answer.
>
> Again the high priest asked him, *"Are you the Christ, the Son of the Blessed One?"*
>
> *"I am," said Jesus. "And you will see the Son of Man sitting at the right hand of the Mighty One and coming on the clouds of heaven."*
>
> *The high priest tore his clothes.* "Why do we need any more witnesses?" he asked. "You have heard the blasphemy. What do you think?"
>
> They all condemned him as worthy of death. *Then some began to spit at him; they blindfolded him, struck him with their fists, and said, "Prophesy!" And the guards took him and beat him.*
>
> (14:53–65)

Who were the Sanhedrin?

The most important rulers of the Temple were the Sanhedrin. They consisted of 70 council members and the High Priest as judge. The Sanhedrin could rule on criminal cases and religious matters. Although they had the power to pass sentence and carry out many of their sentences, this did not include the death penalty. Only the Romans, who ruled the country, were permitted to execute people.

The trial before the Sanhedrin was a preparation for handing Jesus over to the Romans to carry out the death penalty, which the Temple authorities wanted.

A fair trial?

- Jewish law required trials that might involve the death penalty to take place during the hours of daylight, but this one was held at night.

- No clear charges were laid before Jesus; in fact the Sanhedrin was casting around to find some evidence with which to charge Jesus. Jesus was neither officially charged with anything, nor given time to prepare his defence.

- Jewish religious laws required more than one witness to agree that they had heard the defendant speak blasphemy. At this trial the witnesses never agreed.

- According to Jewish law, a person is guilty of blasphemy if they actually use God's name, but Jesus never did.

How does Jesus' trial affect Christians' attitudes to justice?

Because Jesus was never given a fair or legal trial, it has led most Christians to be strong supporters of a fair judicial system.

The abuse and torture Jesus suffered has led some Christians to be outspoken about human rights abuse. Peter Benenson, a Roman Catholic, was not prepared to stand by whilst human rights were infringed; he set up Amnesty International. Since its early beginnings in the 1960s, Amnesty has grown into a worldwide non-religious organization that works to stop human rights abuse and gain justice for anyone who has suffered.

The British Council of Churches, with the support of Amnesty International, formed Action by Christians Against Torture in 1984. The treatment of Jesus after his arrest has made Christians very aware of the horrors and injustice of torture.

This candle burns in the Prisoner of Conscience Chapel at Salisbury Cathedral. It is a symbol of Christians' concern that anyone who is arrested should be treated justly. The candle burns in the centre to remind Christians of the light of Jesus that is never extinguished. The barbed wire represents the crown of thorns rammed down on Jesus' head before his crucifixion. The spikes symbolize the nails that pieced his hands. Find out the link between this candle and the logo of Amnesty International.

Activity 1

Examine the titles Jesus applied to himself during the trial before the High Priest. Explain why they would bring him into conflict with the Sanhedrin.

Activity 2

Look back through the work you did in Chapter 2, collecting evidence about the ways Jesus came into conflict with the authorities. Write a charge sheet against Jesus for the Sanhedrin.

Activity 3

Write a press release on behalf of the Sanhedrin justifying their decision to find Jesus guilty. Make sure you counter any suggestions that their trial was a foregone conclusion and 'just for show'.

 Check you have learnt:

- what the Sanhedrin accused Jesus of
- what evidence the Sanhedrin had
- how Jesus' trial affects Christians' attitudes to justice.

TRY YOUR SKILL AT THIS

The (b) question:

Do you think Jesus should have done more to defend himself in front of the High Priest?

Give **two** reasons for your point of view. (4)

In this topic you will examine the meaning and significance of the trial before Pilate, and consider why Christians today see the significance differently to Mark.

Pontius Pilate the Roman procurator (governor) of Judea at the time of Jesus

The Sanhedrin had no power to execute Jesus, so they had to convince the Romans to do it. Jesus was trussed up like a dangerous criminal when they brought him before the Roman governor.

The Jewish authorities accused Jesus of calling himself 'king of the Jews'. This had political overtones and suggested that Jesus threatened Roman rule.

Mark didn't state what Jesus was accused of, but it had to be political, such as threatening to cause an uprising, because religious issues did not concern Pilate.

Jesus was meek and accepted his fate, making no attempt to protest his innocence. He was fulfilling the prophecy of the Messiah as a suffering servant.

Pilate was aware of the Sanhedrin's mischief and did not believe that Jesus was guilty. He was reluctant to condemn him to death.

The crowd that had previously welcomed Jesus when he entered Jerusalem at the beginning of the week had been manipulated to shout for Jesus' death and the release of the murderer Barabbas.

The background

Palestine, at the time of Jesus, was ruled by the Romans. This meant that the Jews had limited authority in their own country. Whilst the Sanhedrin could hold trials for religious crimes like blasphemy, they were not permitted to carry out the death penalty. Only the Romans could execute people, which they might do for breaking Roman law, but never for breaking religious rules. To ensure that Jesus was permanently removed from the scene, the Sanhedrin needed to convince the Romans that Jesus had broken one of their laws that carried the death penalty. They took Jesus to the Roman governor, **Pontius Pilate**, saying that Jesus was calling himself a king. Such a title was a political threat to Roman power.

> Very early in the morning, the chief priests, with the elders, the teachers of the law and *the whole Sanhedrin, reached a decision. They bound Jesus, led him away and handed him over to Pilate.*
>
> "Are you *the king of the Jews*?" asked Pilate.
>
> "Yes, it is as you say," Jesus replied.
>
> *The chief priests accused him of many things.* So again Pilate asked him, "Aren't you going to answer? See how many things they are accusing you of."
>
> *But Jesus still made no reply*, and Pilate was amazed.
>
> Now it was the custom at the Feast to release a prisoner whom the people requested. A man called Barabbas was in prison with the insurrectionists who had committed murder in the uprising. The crowd came up and asked Pilate to do for them what he usually did.
>
> "Do you want me to release to you the king of the Jews?" asked *Pilate, knowing it was out of envy that the chief priests had handed Jesus over to him. But the chief priests stirred up the crowd to have Pilate release Barabbas instead.*
>
> "What shall I do, then, with the one you call the king of the Jews?" Pilate asked them.
>
> "Crucify him!" they shouted.
>
> "Why? What crime has he committed?" asked Pilate.
>
> **But** *they shouted all the louder, "Crucify him!"*
>
> *Wanting to satisfy the crowd, Pilate released Barabbas to them.* **He had Jesus flogged, and handed him over to be crucified.**
>
> (15:1–15)

Conflicting views of Pontius Pilate

Mark's account portrays Pilate as weak and ineffectual because he was swayed by public opinion. It is clear from the passage that Pilate knew Jesus was innocent and the trial was a sham. The Jewish authorities put forward various charges that Pilate didn't believe because he knew they were based on envy of Jesus' popularity. If you read the passage carefully, you can see that Pilate never made the decision himself. He let the crowd decide what to do with Jesus and who to release, even though he knew the Temple authorities had manipulated the crowd.

Historical evidence about Pilate shows him to have been anything but weak and ineffectual. He had a reputation for dealing out harsh justice. One writer of the period described him as 'inflexible, merciless and obstinate'.

Christians on their knees pray at Lourdes before the first station of the cross, which shows Jesus condemned to death by Pilate. You can see the Romans soldiers in this scene. What religious reasons do you think inspire Christians to go up these steps on their knees?

Activity 1

Compare Jesus' trial before the Sanhedrin with his trial before Pilate. Note the charges, the evidence and the opportunities Jesus had to defend himself. What similarities are there?

Do you think either was an example of a fair trial? Explain why.

Activity 2

Write out the prophecy from Isaiah 53:7–8 about the Messiah being the suffering servant. Underline the words where you think Jesus fulfilled the prophecy of a suffering servant. Briefly write along-side how you think Jesus fulfilled the prophecy.

 He was oppressed and afflicted, yet he did not open his mouth; he was led like a lamb to the slaughter, and as a sheep before her shearers is silent, so he did not open his mouth. By oppression and judgment he was taken away.

(Isaiah 53:7–8)

Mark's view of the trial versus a modern Christian's view of the trial

When it came to deciding who the villains were, Mark decided it was the Jews. He has shown them to be using all sorts of dishonest means to get Jesus convicted of a charge that carried the death penalty. By contrast, the Romans, who were the ones who would carry out the crucifixion, were treated lightly. In this account, Pilate was seen to be very reasonable but weak. He was quite prepared to release Jesus but was influenced by the rabble who shouted for Jesus' crucifixion. Scared of a riot, Pilate bowed to public opinion and condemned an innocent man.

The public were shown to be fickle and easily convinced by whoever shouted the loudest. Those who welcomed Jesus on Palm Sunday now shouted for his death. The Jewish crowd preferred the release of a rabble rouser and convicted murderer to an innocent man of peace.

Mark's approach has influenced some Christians to be anti-Jewish in the past. However, modern Christians view the trial of Jesus slightly differently. They see the event as part of God's plan for the sacrifice of his Son to save humanity from sin and death. Jesus himself was an observant Jew and he taught his followers to treat everyone equally, no matter what their faith or culture.

Archaeologists discovered this stone fragment at Caesarea in the Judea region of Israel, where Pontius Pilate's headquarters were. Its Latin inscription dates from the time of Jesus and translates as: 'This building was built by Pontius Pilate Prefect of Judea.'

✓ **Check you have learnt:**

- what Jesus was charged with when he was brought before Pilate
- how Jesus was treated by Pilate
- how Mark's account could be seen as anti-Jewish
- how modern Christians view this trial.

TRY YOUR SKILL AT THIS

The (c) question:

Explain why some Christians today might see the significance of the trial before Pilate in a different way to Mark. (8)

In this topic you will think about the meaning and significance of the crucifixion in Mark's Gospel.

KEYWORDS KEYWORDS

crucifixion the Roman death penalty suffered by Jesus when he was nailed to the cross

Golgotha the place of the skull; the place where Jesus was crucified

The background

Mark's account of the **crucifixion** gives no details of Jesus' execution; instead it concentrates on the details that surrounded Jesus' crucifixion. Mark wanted his readers to know and understand that Jesus was the Messiah prophesied in the Old Testament: the suffering servant.

> A certain man from Cyrene, Simon, the father of Alexander and Rufus, was passing by on his way in from the country, and they forced him to carry the cross. They brought Jesus to the place called **Golgotha** (which means The Place of the Skull). *Then they offered him wine mixed with myrrh, but he did not take it. And they crucified him. Dividing up his clothes, they cast lots to see what each would get.*
>
> It was the third hour when they crucified him. *The written notice of the charge against him read: THE KING OF THE JEWS. They crucified two robbers with him, one on his right and one on his left. Those who passed by hurled insults at him, shaking their heads* and saying, "So! You who are going to destroy the temple and build it in three days, come down from the cross and save yourself!"
>
> In the same way the chief priests and the teachers of the law mocked him among themselves. "He saved others," they said, "but he can't save himself! Let this Christ, this King of Israel, come down now from the cross, that we may see and believe." Those crucified with him also heaped insults on him.
>
> At the sixth hour darkness came over the whole land until the ninth hour. And at the ninth hour Jesus cried out in a loud voice, *"Eloi, Eloi, lama sabachthani?" – which means, "My God, my God, why have you forsaken me?"*
>
> *When some of those standing near heard this, they said, "Listen, he's calling Elijah."*
>
> One man ran, filled a sponge with wine vinegar, put it on a stick, and offered it to Jesus to drink. "Now leave him alone. Let's see if Elijah comes to take him down," he said.
>
> With a loud cry, Jesus breathed his last.
>
> *The curtain of the temple was torn in two from top to bottom. And when the centurion, who stood there in front of Jesus, heard his cry and saw how he died, he said, "Surely this man was the Son of God!"*
>
> (15:21–39)

A mixture of myrrh and wine was offered to Jesus as a mild anaesthetic to dull the pain. Jesus refused it, showing he was prepared to take the full pain of crucifixion.

Throwing dice to see who would have Jesus' clothes bears out an Old Testament prophecy in Psalm 22:18.

The title 'King of the Jews' had political overtones for the Romans. The Temple authorities certainly did not agree with this title yet, as Messiah, Jesus was the King of Israel and a descendant of King David.

The robbers either side of Jesus showed that, even in death, Jesus was in the midst of sinners and outcasts.

Psalm 22:7 refers to passers-by hurling insults.

Jesus' words in Aramaic are from Psalm 22:1. Jesus may have been using this as a prayer, or perhaps he was crying out in despair believing that God had abandoned him. The word "Eloi" was misheard by bystanders as an appeal to the prophet Elijah to come and help him.

This curtain separated an area called the Holy of Holies (a part of the Temple so sacred only the High Priest was allowed to go in once a year) from the area for ordinary worshippers. Its split showed that Jesus' death had destroyed the barrier between God and humanity.

Mark's account states that it was a Roman soldier, not a Jew, who recognized the real identity of Jesus.

What did Mark want his readers to understand about Jesus' crucifixion?

Mark's account states in a very straightforward way, 'they crucified him'. It does not give details of the crucifixion such as where the nails went or the pain and agony Jesus suffered. The passage shows readers the special significance Jesus' death has for Christians. The details Mark selected demonstrate that Jesus was the Messiah, the suffering servant.

Mark's narrative continually fulfils prophecies about the Messiah in Psalm 22, which Mark's readers would have been familiar with. Mark's 'matter-of-fact' crucifixion account emphasizes Jesus meekly accepting his fate. This is also shown by his refusal to accept the offer of something to dull the pain; Jesus was prepared to endure the full agony of crucifixion to save others.

The words Jesus called out from the cross are from Psalm 22. Those who thought he was calling Elijah remembered the Jewish belief that the prophet Elijah would return to earth just before the arrival of the Messiah. Once again, this enforces Jesus' real identity.

In contrast to the taunts of the chief priests and Jewish teachers, it was a Roman soldier, a non-Jew, who was the first to recognize Jesus' true identity as the Son of God. Some scholars have suggested that Mark was writing his gospel in Rome when early Christians were being persecuted and he wanted to show the Romans in a good light.

This shows Simon of Cyrene being told to carry the cross for Jesus. Although we do not know who Simon was, Mark believed his readers would know him, which is why he added details of the man's family. By doing this, Mark probably felt it would give his story credibility.

Activity 1

Explain how and why Mark's account shows his readers that Jesus was the Messiah who was prophesied in the Old Testament.

Activity 2

Some suggest that Mark deliberately chose what he presented in his account so his readers would understand it in a certain way. When someone selects and presents certain material for effect we often call this 'spin'.

In pairs, discuss whether there is any evidence that Mark did this in his crucifixion account. Make sure you check the story against Psalm 22.

✔ Check you have learnt:

- the details of Jesus' crucifixion
- how Mark used Old Testament references in his account
- what Mark might have been trying to teach his readers about Jesus.

TRY YOUR SKILL AT THIS

The (d) question:

'Because Mark's account of the crucifixion lacks basic details it is not very helpful to Christians.'

In your answer you should refer to Christianity.

(i) Do you agree? Give reasons for your opinion. (3)

(ii) Give reasons why some people may disagree with you. (3)

In this topic you will consider the reasons why the crucifixion is important for Christians today.

The background

The horror of a person being put to death for a crime they haven't committed is bad enough, but the crucifixion of Jesus has far more significance than that for Christians. Without Jesus' death, there would be no Christianity. What we will investigate here are the reasons why Jesus had to die.

Why did Mark say Jesus' death was necessary?

Mark's Gospel gives this reason for Jesus' crucifixion:

 For even the Son of Man did not come to be served, but to serve, and to give his life as a ransom for many.

(10:45)

At the time Mark was writing, slavery was common and the only way out of slavery was for somebody to buy that slave's freedom by paying a ransom.

18 February

Ransom demanded to free hostage

We are familiar with the idea of a ransom being demanded in return for somebody's freedom. Unless money is handed over, the hostage is condemned to death. However, in return for a payment, the hostage is freed and able to live their life.

Because the sins of humanity through the ages are so great, people stand no chance of being able to pay the price of gaining their freedom from death. The price is too high and we are mere humans. Only someone as valuable as God's Son can pay that sort of price. Giving his life would pay the ransom and give humanity the freedom of life after death.

Why did Jesus have to die?

They are many different beliefs about why it was necessary for Jesus to give his life. Modern Christians are less inclined than Christians in the past to accept the idea of a father, in the form of God, demanding that his son be put to death to pay a debt. This is not only cruel, but does not fit in with the idea of the loving Father Jesus taught in the gospels. Twenty-first-century Christians are more likely to consider the idea that Jesus' death on the cross was because he wanted to show them the way back to God.

Original sin

Some Christians believe that the clue to understanding Jesus' crucifixion is here: Adam and Eve, the first people, disobeyed God. Their sin not only caused them to be cast out of the Garden of Eden, but it continued down the generations and separated people from God. There was nothing humans could do alone to make amends for the original sin. It required something far greater to return humans to God. Only someone as perfect as Jesus was great enough to pay the price of humanity's sins and return people to God.

A sacrifice

> This is my blood of the covenant, which is poured out for many.
>
> (14:24)

At the time Mark was writing, Jews were familiar with the idea of killing an animal and offering its blood to God to ask forgiveness for their sins. The idea was to give something of value to God in order to receive something of value in return. The Passover story (pages 70–71) speaks of lambs being sacrificed in the Temple to thank God for the Jews being saved from slavery in Egypt.

Early Christians understood Jesus' death in the same way: a blood price paid to God in return for humanity's sins being forgiven. Offering blood sacrifices to God is not a concept many Christians today feel comfortable with. They might, however, accept that Jesus chose to give his life freely and out of love for all humanity.

Sin separates people from God. By allowing himself to be crucified, Jesus has saved people from the power of sin. The death of Jesus removes the barrier between God and humanity in the same way that the splitting of the Temple curtain took away the divide between God and worshippers.

To abolish death

Some Christians believe that Jesus became human and suffered crucifixion in order to abolish death. They believe that Jesus' willingness to give his life has meant that people have eternal life in heaven with God. Jesus' death led to his resurrection, which has opened the way to life after death for everyone else. It was all part of God's plan.

Activity 1

Create your own diagram to display the different reasons Christians give for the importance of the crucifixion.

This painting of the crucifixion emphasizes the violence of the situation by using sharp jagged images.

Check you have learnt:

- three different reasons Christians might give for Jesus' death
- what is meant by Jesus' death as a ransom
- what Christians have gained from Jesus' death.

If Jesus hadn't died...

Trying to understand the reason why Jesus allowed himself to be put to death still causes Christians difficulties. Some find it more helpful to think about the problem from the opposite direction and ask what would have happened if Jesus hadn't died. Although Jesus could have carried on his ministry for longer, there would have been little to distinguish him from other wandering preachers. Most significantly, without Jesus' death there could be no resurrection. For many modern Christians, this is the reason for his crucifixion.

Activity 2

Explain why some Christians might say that Jesus' death would be meaningless without the resurrection.

TRY YOUR SKILL AT THIS

The (b) question:

Do you think Jesus had to die?

Give **two** reasons for your point of view. (4)

DO YOU KNOW?

Improve your skill with the (a) question

Keyword meanings	Keyword	Mark
Associating oneself with God/language or deeds which insult God.		
The Roman death penalty suffered by Jesus when he was nailed to the cross.		
The supreme Jewish council which found Jesus guilty of blasphemy.		
The Roman procurator (governor) of Judea at the time of Jesus.		
The chief Jewish leader at the time of Jesus.		
The place of the skull; the place where Jesus was crucified.		

✳ TRY THIS ✳

Copy out each of the keyword meanings. Write the correct keyword alongside. Then mark your answers according to the mark scheme on page 24 and the definitions on page 69.

Improve your skill with the (c) question

The topics you have just studied are the meaning and significance of the trial before the High Priest and before Pilate. You have also learnt about the meaning and significance of the crucifixion. These have affected Christian attitudes towards justice so make sure you understand what these attitudes are and can support them with reasons.

Check you can remember the predictions Jesus made about his death and those in the scriptures. Keep these in mind when developing full answers to the (c) questions on these topics because you will be able to use them when explaining the importance of the crucifixion to Christians today.

Try **one** of these (c) questions and don't forget your QWC!

Explain why Christians today believe the crucifixion is important. (8)

Explain why the trial before the High Priest affects Christians' attitude to justice. (8)

Explain why Christians today may understand the significance of the trial before Pilate in a different way to Mark. (8)

STEP 1

Copy out the questions underlining the important words.

STEP 2

Jot down as many points as you can think of.

STEP 3

Develop the points into full sentences and support them with reasons.

WHAT DO YOU THINK?

Improve your skill with the (d) question

Some of the controversial areas in this unit are likely to be about the trial and crucifixion: 'The trial before Pilate was a fix.' This could form the basis of a (b) or a (d) question because it is challenging you to reply.

You could answer it considering the way Mark explained it, or you could think about Pilate's motives or even those of the Sanhedrin who brought Jesus before Pilate. These considerations could give you several alternative view points to discuss or evidence to support your own opinion.

Try out your answer to this statement as a (d) question:

> 'The trial before Pilate was a fix.'
> In your answer you should refer to Christianity.
> (i) Do you agree? Give reasons for your opinion. (3)
> (ii) Give reasons why some people may disagree with you. (3)

Gavin wrote:

> (i) I don't think it was a fix. I think it is more likely that Pilate was weak and got pushed around by people. He did what the Sanhedrin wanted. You have only got to look at the way he asked the crowd what they wanted and obeyed even though he knew Jesus was innocent.
> (ii) Others might say it was a fix because the Sanhedrin had set Jesus up.

Can you add any more to Gavin's answer? His second part starts well but he doesn't give any reasons. Please complete it aiming at a Level 4 grade.

Another controversial area is whether the crucifixion has any relevance today. When answering a question like this you might find it helpful to tackle the issue from the other direction. Ask yourself: if Jesus had not been crucified at all what difference would it make to Christians at the time and today. You can probably see with this example that if it hadn't happened things would have turned out very differently. 'There would be no Christianity because...': can you supply **two** reasons?

Here is a (d) question:

> 'The crucifixion happened two thousand years ago, it is not relevant today.'
> In your answer you should refer to Christianity.
> (i) Do you agree? Give reasons for your opinion. (3)
> (ii) Give reasons why some people may disagree with you. (3)

Yogita wrote this:

> Two thousand years ago is a long time and most people don't take any notice of things that old. Mark might have got it wrong anyway. Christians can't be sure, can they? I am a Christian and I believe in the crucifixion because I think the resurrection is important. I wouldn't be able to go to heaven if Jesus hadn't risen from the dead.

Look closely at Yogita's answer, which has muddled everything up. Can you find an answer to part (i)? What sort of reasons has she given? Is there material for part (ii)? Has Yogita included any reasons?

Compare Yogita's answer with the marking grid on page 25. How many marks does she score?

In this topic you will learn about the meaning and significance of the burial for Christians today.

The background

Details of Jesus' burial become very important if Christians are going to accept Jesus' resurrection. This is even more important for modern Christians who live in an age that demands proof. If there is any evidence that Jesus was not really dead, or that his followers were unsure which tomb he had been buried in, then the resurrection is in doubt. If that were the case, it would undermine everything Christianity is based on.

The exam paper does not require that you study the following gospel passage like the others included in this book, but it is very helpful for you to examine it for evidence of Jesus' death and burial.

> It was Preparation Day (that is, the day before the Sabbath). So as evening approached, Joseph of Arimathea, a prominent member of the Council, who was himself waiting for the kingdom of God, went boldly to Pilate and asked for Jesus' body. Pilate was surprised to hear that he was already dead. Summoning the centurion, he asked him if Jesus had already died. When he learned from the centurion that it was so, he gave the body to Joseph. So Joseph bought some linen cloth, took down the body, wrapped it in the linen, and placed it in a tomb cut out of rock. Then he rolled a stone against the entrance of the tomb. Mary Magdalene and Mary the mother of Jesus saw where he was laid.
>
> **(15:42–47)**

Mark's Gospel states that Jesus was the Son of God who died and then came back to life three days later. Modern Christians may seek more reassurance than early Christians that the events really happened like this. This is because today we have been educated to examine evidence carefully before we accept it.

What facts come from Mark's account of the burial?

Mark's account states that the body was removed from the cross at the end of the day and taken for burial. Normally the bodies of criminals would have been left hanging there as a warning to others, but in Jesus' case a special request was made to Pilate.

What is unusual about the request is that it came from Joseph of Arimathea, a leading member of the Sanhedrin, the very group that had Jesus arrested and handed over to Pilate after a sham trial. This suggests that the Sanhedrin was not totally united against Jesus.

Once permission was granted, Joseph purchased a burial cloth to wrap the body in and placed it in a rock tomb. The witnesses to this burial were Jesus' mother Mary and Mary Magdalene, a close supporter of Jesus.

Activity 1

Script the conversation Joseph of Arimathea had with Pilate when he asked for Jesus' body.

This ancient tomb in Jerusalem is cut into the rock. Once the body was placed inside the tomb a rock was rolled in front and the tomb sealed. Jesus was placed in a tomb like this.

Was Jesus really dead?

In Mark's account Pilate expressed surprise that Jesus was dead. This is because victims of crucifixion often had a slow lingering death, which lasted for a couple of days. The victim would eventually die when their arms gave out and could no longer take their weight on the cross. The body would slump down causing congestion in the lungs, and suffocation. A strong person could usually manage to prop themselves up for more than a day. In Mark 15 he refers to Jesus being flogged before his crucifixion. This form of torture with a leather whip containing sharp metal spikes was likely to have severely weakened Jesus before he was nailed to the cross.

What is useful in Mark's account of Jesus' burial is that it mentions several witnesses who saw Jesus dead. The most notable was the Roman centurion whom Pilate consulted. This man would have been used to crucifixions and would be able to assess whether or not the victim was dead. If he had made a mistake when telling Pilate, he was likely to have paid for this with his own life. Also, as a non-Jew, the Roman centurion had no personal interest in the victim so his testimony is likely to have been impartial and accurate.

The passage also states that Joseph of Arimathea, Jesus' mother Mary and Mary Magdalene were present when the body was taken down from the cross. They were also witnesses to Jesus' death.

Confirming Jesus was dead when he was buried was important to Mark, because without that evidence the resurrection would appear a sham.

Just as important, Mark must convince his readers that at least one of the women knew exactly where Jesus was buried. This matters when the women returned to the tomb three days later and found Jesus gone. Mark's readers have to know the women would not have made the mistake of going to the wrong tomb.

Activity 2

List the factual evidence modern Christians might use to support their view that Jesus' death and resurrection really happened.

This scene at Lourdes depicts Jesus being placed in the tomb supplied by Joseph of Arimathea.

Check you have learnt:

- what happened after Jesus was crucified
- what evidence there was that Jesus was really dead
- why it matters that modern Christians believe in the burial story.

What is the meaning of the burial for modern Christians?

Mark's account of the burial of Jesus contains the sort of evidence that provides modern Christians with proof that Jesus really was dead. Without that proof the resurrection would be invalid. The fact that Jesus rose again from the dead gives heart to modern Christians that Jesus will keep his word and they will join him in heaven after they die.

The presence of Joseph of Arimathea is also significant. Although Joseph was a member of the Sanhedrin, some Christians have suggested he was not present when the vote was taken about whether or not Jesus was guilty. Mark's account mentions that Joseph 'was himself waiting for the kingdom of God'. The fact that Joseph was breaking Jewish Sabbath rules by buying a burial cloth and placing the body in the tomb after the Sabbath had started suggests that this important Jewish leader accepted that Jesus was the Messiah.

TRY YOUR SKILL AT THIS

The (b) question:

Do you think there is enough evidence to prove that Jesus was actually dead when he was placed in the tomb?

Give **two** reasons for your point of view. (4)

3.10

The resurrection

In this topic you will consider the meaning and significance of the resurrection as recorded by Mark.

The background

Jesus' body had been hurriedly buried without being correctly washed or anointed with spices according to Jewish ritual. This was because the Sabbath was about to begin and Jewish law requires all work to cease at Sabbath. As soon as the Sabbath was over the women closest to Jesus returned to put things right and give him the correct burial. They came very early in the morning because they were unsure whether they ought to be there.

Mary Magdalene was also present when Jesus was taken down from the cross and buried (see pages 90–91).

The large rock that sealed the entrance, which the three women feared would be too heavy to move, had been pushed aside.

The young man in white is not explained, but many Christians believe this refers to an angel, a messenger from God, sitting in the tomb.

This was the first sign that Jesus, who was dead, had been resurrected: his body had gone from the tomb.

The women were invited to look in the tomb and witness for themselves that the body had gone.

Jesus had prophesied that when he rose from the dead they would find him in Galilee.

> **When the Sabbath was over,** *Mary Magdalene,* **Mary the mother of James, and Salome bought spices so that they might go to anoint Jesus' body. Very early on the first day of the week, just after sunrise, they were on their way to the tomb and they asked each other, "Who will roll the stone away from the entrance of the tomb?"**
>
> *But when they looked up, they saw that the stone, which was very large, had been rolled away.* **As they entered the tomb,** *they saw a young man dressed in a white robe sitting on the right side, and they were alarmed.*
>
> **"Don't be alarmed," he said.** *"You are looking for Jesus the Nazarene, who was crucified. He has risen! He is not here. See the place where they laid him.* **But go, tell his disciples and Peter,** *'He is going ahead of you into Galilee. There you will see him, just as he told you.'"*
>
> **Trembling and bewildered, the women went out and fled from the tomb. They said nothing to anyone, because they were afraid.**
>
> (16:1–8)

Providing the evidence

Mark knew that Jesus had indeed risen from the dead and his account contains evidence which he believed would convince others that the miracle had taken place. For this reason, his account contains quite a few verifiable pieces of information.

There are three witnesses to the empty tomb, which prevents anyone suggesting this story is the result of one person's fantasy. One of the women, Mary Magdalene, also saw Jesus' dead body late on the Friday when it was taken down from the cross. She had no doubt he was dead because she was present when the body was put in the tomb. Having seen the huge rock pushed in front of the entrance, she was concerned that the three women would not have the strength to roll the stone back.

Mark's account is very precise about the time they witnessed the empty tomb. It was early on the Sabbath. It is described as just after sunrise on the first day of the week, which in Judaism is Sunday.

The three women were also invited by the angel to look in the tomb and see with their own eyes that Jesus' body had gone. Once again, eyewitness statements from three people are powerful evidence.

What is the significance of Mark's account of the resurrection?

The oldest manuscripts of Mark's Gospel end with this account. Later copies of the gospel, which are likely to have had an extended ending added by other writers, take the story of the resurrection further. Mark, it seems, felt his task was over at chapter 16 verse 8. He had given his readers evidence that Jesus had risen from the dead, exactly fulfilling all of the prophecies.

The young man in white in the tomb is understood to be an angel. This means that God sent a messenger to the women to tell them that his only Son had risen from the dead. Having seen an angel give this amazing message, it is not surprising that the women were terrified and bewildered.

The angel's message had great significance. He told them:

- the crucified Jesus had risen. This is exactly as Jesus had told his disciples and in the same three-day time frame
- to take the message to the disciples and to Peter. Jesus' special relationship with Peter was recognized when the angel named him specifically
- Jesus was already waiting for them in Galilee. As this is many miles from Jerusalem, it proved that Jesus' body was not the same weak and crucified one they saw on the Friday. They would be able to see him in the flesh.

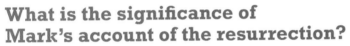

This altar painting attempts to capture the whole resurrection story in one picture. Roman guards are terrified as Jesus arises in glory before the women come around the corner of the rock tomb.

For Christians, the empty cross is a symbol of Jesus' resurrection.

Activity 1

Write Mary Magdalene's blog, giving her own account of why she went to the tomb on Sunday morning and what she saw there. Most people are likely to dismiss Mary's words as the delusions of a distraught woman; therefore, she needs to provide convincing evidence that she is telling the truth.

✓ Check you have learnt:

- what happened when the women arrived at the tomb
- what evidence there is for the resurrection
- the significance of the angel's message.

TRY YOUR SKILL AT THIS

The (d) question:

'The evidence for Jesus' resurrection is not convincing.'

In your answer you should refer to Christianity.

(i) Do you agree? Give reasons for your opinion. (3)

(ii) Give reasons why some people may disagree with you. (3)

Why does the resurrection have significance for Christians today?

In this topic you will examine the meaning and significance of the resurrection for Christians today.

Useful specialist language

salvation people are saved from their sins and brought closer to God through Jesus' death and resurrection

The background

The resurrection is the basis of Christianity. If Jesus did not rise again from the dead, then for 2000 years Christians have been following a fraud and, more significantly, there would be no life after death. The difficulty for modern Christians is that the resurrection goes against everything they have ever witnessed. We need to investigate how modern Christians come to terms with something that defies science.

The problem of the resurrection

Twenty-first-century Christians have problems with the resurrection story. The idea of someone coming back to life three days after they have been pronounced dead goes against human experience. No one has ever done that. Some might argue that advances in medical technology and reports of near-death experiences could make the idea of Jesus' resurrection more likely today than in the first century.

When early Christians had problems accepting that Jesus had risen from the dead, the apostle St Paul wrote the following letter to them. He argued that, logically, the resurrection must have taken place:

> If there is no resurrection of the dead, then not even Christ has been raised. And if Christ has not been raised, our preaching is useless and so is your faith. More than that, we are then found to be false witnesses about God, for we have testified about God that he raised Christ from the dead. But he did not raise him if in fact the dead are not raised.
>
> **(1 Corinthians 15:13-15)**

Evidence for the resurrection

One problem is that nobody saw the resurrection happen. A detective might say the evidence is circumstantial. The women who arrived at the tomb, where they believed Jesus was buried, found it empty. Jesus had told them that he would rise again in three days and the time was right. The women saw an angel who told them that Jesus had risen.

Mark's Gospel ends here but St Paul said he had evidence that Jesus had appeared to many of his followers in the days after the resurrection:

Activity 1

a) Analyse St Paul's words and write down why he said the resurrection is at the heart of Christian beliefs.

b) Belief in the resurrection is still at the heart of Christianity 2000 years later. What do you think Paul might say about this?

> ...he appeared to Peter, and then to the Twelve. After that, he appeared to more than five hundred of the brothers at the same time, most of whom are still living, though some have fallen asleep. Then he appeared to James, then to all the apostles, and last of all he appeared to me also...
>
> **(1 Corinthians 15:5–8)**

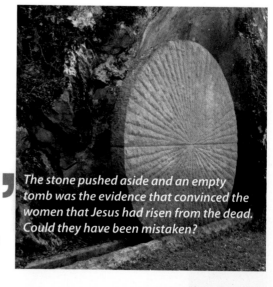

The stone pushed aside and an empty tomb was the evidence that convinced the women that Jesus had risen from the dead. Could they have been mistaken?

One or two people might have imagined they saw Jesus: is it likely that so many people could have made a mistake?

What the resurrection means for other Christians

Some modern Christians do not think the story of Jesus' resurrection should be taken literally at all. They argue that after Jesus' death the disciples came to realize exactly who he was and this inspired them to continue his work. This inspiration was so strong that many of Jesus' followers have been prepared to die for their beliefs, as Jesus died for them.

To support their case, they quote St Paul who also said that resurrection is a spiritual thing:

> But someone may ask, "How are the dead raised? With what kind of body will they come?" How foolish! What you sow does not come to life unless it dies. When you sow, you do not plant the body that will be, but just a seed, perhaps of wheat or of something else.
>
> **(1 Corinthians 15:35–37)**
>
> So will it be with the resurrection of the dead. The body that is sown is perishable, it is raised imperishable; it is sown in dishonour, it is raised in glory; it is sown in weakness, it is raised in power; it is sown a natural body, it is raised a spiritual body. If there is a natural body, there is also a spiritual body.
>
> **(1 Corinthians 42–44)**

A former Bishop of Durham caused controversy in the 1980s when he said that the resurrection was more than a conjuring trick with bones.

Some Christians found his choice of words offensive but what the Bishop was telling modern Christians was that they should concern themselves with the significance of the resurrection rather than spend their time worrying whether it happened exactly as described in the Gospels.

What is the significance of the resurrection to Christians today?

Belief in Jesus rising from the dead is central to Christianity. It forms part of the Creed, which many Christians recite in their Sunday worship.

> I believe … in Jesus Christ, his only Son, our Lord … Who was crucified, died and was buried. He descended into hell. The third day he rose again from the dead.
>
> …I believe in the resurrection of the body and the life everlasting.

Christians believe that Jesus' resurrection paves the way for their own. Jesus told his followers that death was not the end and they would enjoy eternal life with him.

For Christians, Jesus' resurrection is proof that he was the Son of God. No ordinary human has been able to return from the dead after three days, so it proves Jesus had divine power.

The death and resurrection of Jesus were part of God's plan for people's salvation. People can be forgiven for their sins and have a life after death in heaven with Jesus.

Even Christians who do not believe that the resurrection happened exactly as it is described still understand that Jesus is more than a person who lived 2000 years ago. They understand that the resurrection story teaches Christians that Jesus is alive and with them in spirit every day.

What is the point of believing in something you can't prove?

Activity 2

What answer would you give to the question above?

Activity 3

a) Draw two columns on your page: one headed FOR, the other AGAINST. In the correct column, write the reasons why some Christians believe or don't believe in the resurrection story.

b) Explain what you believe happened and your reasons.

✓ Check you have learnt:

- why some Christians believe the resurrection happened
- why other Christians do not take the story literally
- three reasons why the resurrection is significant to Christians today.

TRY YOUR SKILL AT THIS

The (b) question:

Do you think Jesus' resurrection was impossible?

Give **two** reasons for your point of view. (4)

SKILLS COACHING 9

END OF CHAPTER 3 CHECK

Check the (a) question

In this chapter about **Death and resurrection** you have learnt these **KEYWORDS**:

- blasphemy
- crucifixion
- Feast of Unleavened Bread
- Gethsemane
- Golgotha
- High Priest
- Judas Iscariot
- Last Supper
- Passover
- Pontius Pilate
- Sanhedrin
- upper room

a) Choose three keywords from the list and explain what they mean.

b) Which three keywords did you not want to choose? Write down what you think their meanings might be and check them. Or, if you really don't know, look them up in the chapter and write down their meanings. It's better to face the difficult keywords now!

Check the (c) question

Make sure that you understand:

- the meaning and significance of the Last Supper for Mark and for Christians today
- the significance of the prayers in Gethsemane and the problems they raise
- the betrayal and trials of Jesus and the issues these raise
- the meaning and significance of the crucifixion for Mark and for Christians today
- the meaning and significance of the resurrection for Mark and for Christians today.

Check the (b) and (d) questions

Check you know different people's responses to the issues above for the (b) and (d) questions.

Remind yourself of two or three reasons the other side gives to argue against you.

Obviously, your responses to the issues above are the most important ones. Rehearse two or three reasons you would give to support your viewpoint on each issue.

Finally, the vitally important thing: how are you going to link it to Mark's Gospel? How could a Christian put that teaching into practice?

Here is a typical example of how questions about *Death and resurrection* might be presented on the exam paper. Choose one of these questions to work through in exam conditions in order to check your progress.

SECTION 3 – DEATH AND RESURRECTION
You must answer ONE question from this section.

EITHER

5 (a) Who was **Judas Iscariot**?　(2)

　(b) Do you think Jesus was actually dead when he was buried?
　　Give **two** reasons for your point of view.　(4)

　(c) Explain why the resurrection is significant for Christians today.　(8)

　(d) 'The Last Supper is more important to Christians today than it was to Mark.'
　　In your answer you should refer to Christianity.
　　(i)　Do you agree? Give reasons for your opinion.　(3)
　　(ii) Give reasons why some people may disagree with you.　(3)
　　　　　　　(Total for Question 5 = 20 marks)

OR

6 (a) What was the **Sanhedrin**?　(2)

　(b) Do you think Jesus' resurrection really happened?
　　Give **two** reasons for your point of view.　(4)

　(c) Explain why there are different attitudes towards Judas amongst Christians today.　(8)

　(d) 'The crucifixion had to happen.'
　　In your answer you should refer to Christianity.
　　(i)　Do you agree? Give reasons for your opinion.　(3)
　　(ii) Give reasons why some people may disagree with you.　(3)
　　　　　　　(Total for Question 6 = 20 marks)

If this had been the real exam, how well would you have done? Use the marking grid to check your progress. Answers to (a) appear on page 69, the grid for (b) is on page 25, the grid for (c) is on page 24 and the grid for (d) is on page 25.

CHAPTER 4

The identity of Jesus

baptism confessing sins and being immersed in water as a sign of purification

confession an acknowledgement or declaration of something

Elijah the Old Testament prophet believed to return before the Messiah

healing miracle a miracle in which Jesus shows his power over sickness

Jairus the synagogue ruler whose daughter was brought back to life by Jesus

John the Baptist the man who baptized Jesus in the river Jordan

Legion a man from whom Jesus cast out many demons

Messiah the Anointed One (Christ) who would bring in God's Kingdom

Moses the Old Testament prophet to whom God gave his laws

nature miracle a miracle in which Jesus shows his power over nature

Son of Man a title used by Jesus of himself, probably meaning he would suffer before bringing in God's Kingdom

transfiguration when Jesus' appearance was changed

What does the baptism story show about Jesus?

In this topic you will look at what the baptism shows about Jesus for Mark and why it causes problems for some Christians today.

KEYWORDS KEYWORD

baptism confessing sins and being immersed in water as a sign of purification

John the Baptist the man who baptized Jesus in the river Jordan

The background

The account of Jesus' **baptism** starts Mark's Gospel. It is very important because it tells readers about Jesus' identity and it signals the beginning of his ministry.

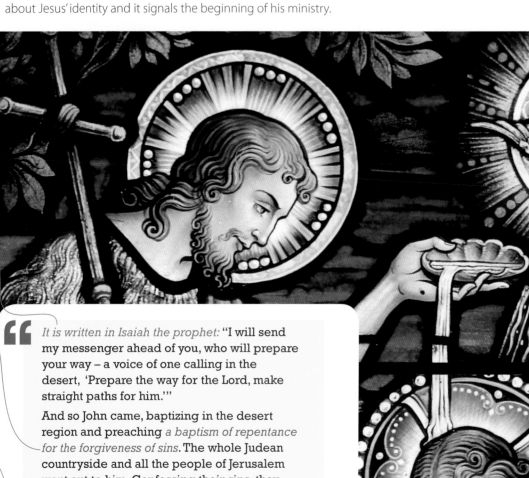

This event was foretold in the scriptures, so it is of great significance.

Water was traditionally a way of showing that a person could be cleansed of sins if they repented and asked for God's forgiveness.

Although **John the Baptist** was recognized as a powerful preacher, he wanted his followers to know he was not the Messiah, only the messenger; Jesus was the real Messiah.

Baptizing with water was a small preparation for something far greater that Jesus would do.

The dove descending on Jesus was a visual sign of God blessing his Son with the power of the Holy Spirit for the ministry Jesus was about to start.

God acknowledged Jesus' identity as his Son with great affection.

> *It is written in Isaiah the prophet:* "I will send my messenger ahead of you, who will prepare your way – a voice of one calling in the desert, 'Prepare the way for the Lord, make straight paths for him.'"
>
> And so John came, baptizing in the desert region and preaching *a baptism of repentance for the forgiveness of sins*. The whole Judean countryside and all the people of Jerusalem went out to him. Confessing their sins, they were baptised by him in the Jordan River. John wore clothing made of camel's hair, with a leather belt around his waist, and he ate locusts and wild honey. And this was his message: "*After me will come one more powerful than I, the thongs of whose sandals I am not worthy to stoop down and untie. I baptise you with water, but he will baptise you with the Holy Spirit.*"
>
> At that time Jesus came from Nazareth in Galilee and was baptised by John in the Jordan. As Jesus was coming up out of the water, he saw heaven being torn open and the *Spirit descending on him like a dove.* And a voice came from heaven: *"You are my Son, whom I love; with you I am well pleased."*
>
> (1:2–11)

Why is the baptism of Jesus important?

Mark's account of Jesus' baptism shows Christians that Jesus is the Son of God. Not only did the voice from heaven recognize Jesus with great love, but God also used this moment to give his Son the special powers of the Holy Spirit. By allowing himself to be baptized by John, Jesus was fulfilling the prophecies in the scriptures and setting an example to his followers.

Why does the baptism of Jesus cause problems for some Christians today?

Was Jesus sinful?

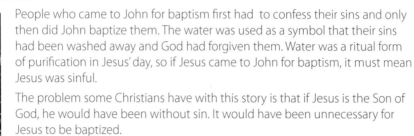

People who came to John for baptism first had to confess their sins and only then did John baptize them. The water was used as a symbol that their sins had been washed away and God had forgiven them. Water was a ritual form of purification in Jesus' day, so if Jesus came to John for baptism, it must mean Jesus was sinful.

The problem some Christians have with this story is that if Jesus is the Son of God, he would have been without sin. It would have been unnecessary for Jesus to be baptized.

In Mark's Gospel, Jesus' baptism is used to symbolize the start of his ministry.

Some Christians choose to be baptized by total immersion in a river because they believe Jesus was baptized that way in the river Jordan. Jesus' baptism marked a significant moment in his life and ministry. What would a Christian say their baptism signifies for them?

Activity 1

Draw a diagram to show:

a) what John said about Jesus

b) what Jesus' baptism shows about his identity.

Activity 2

Script a dialogue between two Christians. One person is talking about the problems they have with this baptism story whilst the other explains what they think the story really means.

Activity 3

a) Research an infant baptism ceremony.

b) Write a piece for a parish magazine explaining what parts of an infant ceremony are linked to Jesus' baptism.

✓ Check you have learnt:

- what happened when Jesus was baptized
- the meaning of the symbolism in the story
- what problems that can raise for Christians today.

TRY YOUR SKILL AT THIS

The (c) question:

Explain why the baptism of Jesus causes problems for some Christians today. (8)

101

Peter's confession at Caesarea Philippi

In this topic you will examine what Peter's confession at Caesarea Philippi shows about Jesus and then consider why Matthew's record of this event is more important for Roman Catholic Christians than Mark's.

KEYWORDS KEYWORDS

Messiah the Anointed One (Christ) who would bring in God's kingdom

confession an acknowledgement or declaration of something

The background

This incident is the turning point in Mark's Gospel. It is significant because Peter recognized Jesus' identity as the Christ, another name for the **Messiah**. The passage is also important because it is the first of three occasions when Jesus predicted his suffering as the Son of Man.

Mark's account of Peter's confession

> Jesus and his disciples went on to the villages around Caesarea Philippi. On the way he asked them, "Who do people say I am?"
>
> They replied, *"Some say John the Baptist; others say Elijah; and still others, one of the prophets."*
>
> "But what about you?" he asked. *"Who do you say I am?"*
>
> Peter answered, *"You are the Christ."*
>
> Jesus warned them not to tell anyone about him.
>
> *He then began to teach them that the Son of Man must suffer many things and be rejected by the elders, chief priests and teachers of the law, and that he must be killed and after three days rise again.* He spoke plainly about this, and Peter took him aside and began to rebuke him.
>
> But when Jesus turned and looked at his disciples, he rebuked Peter. "Get behind me, Satan!" he said. *"You do not have in mind the things of God, but the things of men."*
>
> **(8:27–33)**

People knew Jesus was special, but they thought he was a prophet, a messenger from God, not God's Son.

Other people's opinions did not matter; it was the disciples' opinions that were important.

Peter used the Greek name for Messiah, which is 'the Christ', so Peter did seem to understand Jesus' role. Jesus told all of the disciples to keep the information to themselves.

Jesus predicted his Passion and death.

When Peter heard the suffering servant view of the Messiah, he told Jesus he was wrong. It was then evident that, despite Jesus' teachings, Peter had not understood Jesus as the Messiah at all and Jesus told him off harshly.

Matthew's account of Peter's confession

> When Jesus came to the region of Caesarea Philippi, he asked his disciples, *"Who do people say the Son of Man is?"*
>
> *They replied, "Some say John the Baptist; others say Elijah; and still others, Jeremiah or one of the prophets."*
>
> "But what about you?" he asked. "Who do you say I am?"
>
> Simon Peter answered, *"You are the Christ, the Son of the living God."*
>
> Jesus replied, *"Blessed are you, Simon son of Jonah, for this was not revealed to you by man, but by my Father in heaven. And I tell you that you are Peter, and on this rock I will build my church, and the gates of Hades will not overcome it. I will give you the keys of the kingdom of heaven;* whatever you bind on earth will be bound in heaven, and whatever you loose on earth will be loosed in heaven." Then he warned his disciples not to tell anyone that he was the Christ.
>
> **(Matthew 16:13–20)**

Jesus gave himself the title 'Son of Man', but the people suggested the names of different prophets, or messengers from God.

Peter used the name 'Christ', which is another name for the Messiah, and added that Jesus is God's Son.

Jesus blessed Peter because he had understood fully who Jesus was. Jesus reduced Simon Peter's name to Peter, which means 'a rock', and told him that Peter would be the founder of Jesus' church on earth and that he would also have authority in heaven.

What did Peter confess?

The word '**confession**' means a declaration of the truth. We are used to hearing about criminals making a confession and in that context we understand they are telling the truth about a situation. Peter was doing the same. When Jesus asked him, "Who do you say I am?" Peter said what he believed to be true, "You are the Christ". This was a significant moment for the Twelve because this was the first time that Jesus had asked his disciples for their views and Peter was the first person to recognize Jesus' identity.

'Christ' is the Greek word for 'Messiah' and Jesus knew there were differing views about the Messiah. Whilst Jesus' interpretation of Messiah is that of the suffering servant foretold by Isaiah, most Jews were looking for a warlord who would overthrow the Romans. Knowing how dangerous this idea was, Jesus told the disciples to keep his identity secret.

The rock in the centre of this church is said to be the one where Jesus (according to Matthew's Gospel) told Peter that he was the rock on which Jesus would build his church.

Activity 1

Draw two columns, or a Venn diagram, to record where Matthew's and Mark's accounts of Peter's confession overlap and differ.

Activity 2

What did Peter confess and why is it so significant?

How does Matthew's version of this story differ from Mark's?

In Matthew's version of the story, Jesus showed greater pleasure at Peter's reply to his question and declared that Peter would become the founder of Jesus' church on earth. Peter would also be given the keys to the kingdom of heaven. This was an honour that was never given to any of the other disciples and showed Jesus' great love for this disciple, the only one who had fully understood Jesus' mission.

Why is this important to Roman Catholics?

Roman Catholics believe that Matthew's account tells them that Peter was the founder of the Christian Church. They regard him as the first pope and all subsequent popes, including Pope Benedict XVI, are true successors to Peter.

Because Matthew's account states that Jesus had given Peter the keys to heaven, Catholics believe that all popes have been given the keys and have the same power to forgive sins that Jesus gave to Peter.

Jesus gave Peter the keys to the kingdom of heaven.

Check you have learnt:

- what is meant by Peter's confession
- the difference between Mark's and Matthew's accounts
- why Matthew's account is important to Roman Catholics.

TRY YOUR SKILL AT THIS

The (b) question:

Do you think there is any difference between Matthew's and Mark's stories of Peter's confession? (4)

In this topic you will study Mark's account of the transfiguration of Jesus to understand what it shows and then consider why it causes problems for some Christians today.

Elijah the Old Testament prophet believed to return before the Messiah

Moses the Old Testament prophet to whom God gave his laws

transfiguration when Jesus' appearance was changed

The background

This event took place six days after Peter's confession. Mark used it to give his readers further evidence of Jesus' identity.

These were the three closest disciples. Going up a high mountain symbolized them becoming closer to God.

It was said that the Prophet **Elijah** would arrive on earth again before the Messiah. **Moses** received the Ten Commandments from God on Mount Sinai. Jesus met and talked with these great prophets.

Mark's readers would be familiar with the idea of God's voice coming out of a cloud. It happened when Moses was given the Ten Commandments by God.

God used similar words to those at Jesus' baptism.

Once again, Jesus emphasized secrecy about this.

The disciples still did not understand Jesus' resurrection.

> And he said to them, "I tell you the truth, some who are standing here will not taste death before they see the kingdom of God come with power."
>
> **After six days** *Jesus took Peter, James and John with him and led them up a high mountain,* where they were all alone. There he was transfigured before them. His clothes became dazzling white, whiter than anyone in the world could bleach them. *And there appeared before them Elijah and Moses, who were talking with Jesus.*
>
> Peter said to Jesus, "Rabbi, it is good for us to be here. Let us put up three shelters – one for you, one for Moses and one for Elijah." (He did not know what to say, they were so frightened.)
>
> *Then a cloud appeared and enveloped them, and a voice came from the cloud: "This is my Son, whom I love. Listen to him!"*
>
> Suddenly, when they looked around, they no longer saw anyone with them except Jesus.
>
> As they were coming down the mountain, *Jesus gave them orders not to tell anyone what they had seen until the Son of Man had risen from the dead.* They kept the matter to themselves, *discussing what "rising from the dead" meant.*
>
> (9:1–10)

These two mosaic panels on the front of the Basilica at Lourdes show the transfiguration of Jesus. Jesus shines out in glory from one, whilst the other less colourful one shows the three disciples kneeling together looking up at Jesus. Behind them stand the Old Testament prophets, Moses and Elijah.

What did the transfiguration mean to Mark?

'**Transfiguration**' is a term meaning that Jesus was transformed mystically. When he stood on the mountain top his clothes became shining white and alongside him appeared two long-dead prophets.

Mark's account contains much symbolism, so his readers are in no doubt that this was a significant event in Jesus' life on earth. The account begins with Jesus taking his three closest disciples up a mountain. In the Old Testament, mountains were places where people drew closer to God; Moses went up a mountain to receive the Ten Commandments from God, who then spoke to him out of a cloud.

The prophets who appeared alongside Jesus were important. Moses represented the old Law God gave to him and Elijah represented the prophet who foretold the coming of the Messiah. Mark wanted his readers to see that Jesus, as the Messiah, fulfilled both the law and the prophets; Jesus represented the new covenant, or bond, between God and humanity.

The story gives Mark's readers a better understanding that Jesus was divine. This is shown not just in what the story says happened but in the links to the Old Testament. The words God used when he spoke were similar to those spoken at Jesus' baptism (see page 100). This made the transfiguration a form of spiritual baptism.

Some Christians have wondered whether Mark believed Jesus was trying to give his disciples an idea of the resurrection that would follow. If so, he failed because the disciples didn't understand. Mark's account ends with the disciples discussing what the resurrection meant.

What problems does the transfiguration cause for Christians today?

Taking an incident like this literally is extremely difficult for modern Christians who need proof. The description of the transfiguration, with visions on mountain tops and people appearing in shining white, seems to go against the laws of nature and this would cause many modern-day Christians problems.

On the one hand, these three disciples had this amazing vision yet, on the other hand, when Jesus was arrested and killed, the disciples vanished. Although they heard God's voice proclaiming Jesus as his Son, they were not convinced of his resurrection. Other Christians have questioned how the disciples would have been able to identify Elijah and Moses: prophets who had been dead for centuries.

Although some Christians do find the story difficult to understand, they draw comfort from the fact that Peter didn't understand what was going on either. Mark's account states that Peter made some odd comments about putting up a shrine for each of the three men, largely because he didn't know what to say.

Christians who take the account of the transfiguration at face value have no problem with it because they believe God is all-powerful. Just because we cannot understand how it happened doesn't mean it was impossible. All things are possible for God.

Other Christians look at what Mark was trying to tell his readers in this account. They understand that he was giving them further evidence that Jesus was the Son of God. This was demonstrated by the words of God at Jesus' baptism and at this, Jesus' spiritual baptism. Jesus as the Messiah was also reinforced with links to the Old Testament showing that Jesus was the one foretold by prophets.

Activity 1

Draw a diagram or create a poster to show the similarities between Jesus' baptism (see page 100) and his transfiguration.

Activity 2

a) Write a contribution to a Bible website explaining why modern Christians have problems with the transfiguration story.

b) Post a reply from a Christian who has no problem with it.

 Check you have learnt:

- what happened at the transfiguration
- what the people who Jesus met symbolized
- why some Christians have problems with this story.

TRY YOUR SKILL AT THIS

The (d) question:

'The story of the transfiguration is a problem for Christians today.'

In your answer you should refer to Christianity.

(i) Do you agree? Give reasons for your opinion. (3)

(ii) Give reasons why some people may disagree with you. (3)

SKILLS COACHING 10

DO YOU KNOW?

Improve your skill with the (a) question

Write out the meaning of each of these from memory:

| baptism (page 100) | John the Baptist (page 100) | confession (page 102) | Messiah (page 102) |

| Moses (page 104) | Elijah (page 104) | transfiguration (page 104) |

Check back in the section and mark your answers according to the mark scheme on page 24.

> ✳ TRY THIS ✳
>
> Work with a partner and each select four keywords and meanings from earlier chapters in this textbook. Make them difficult! In fact, choose the four that you found the hardest to remember because, by doing so, it will help you to fix their meanings in your mind. Now challenge your partner to give you the correct definition. Swap round and see who wins. You can play it as a class game if you prefer.

Improve your skill with the (c) question

Try this (c) question:

> **Explain why the transfiguration causes problems for Christians today.** (8)

Remember the step-by-step approach?

STEP 1

Underline the important words in the question.

STEP 2

Draw two columns on your page. Here, you need one column to put what Mark says happened. The other column is for reasons why some Christians today cannot accept the story at face value. Aim for two or three ways in which today's Christians interpret the story.

STEP 3

Write up each reason as a full sentence with a good explanation – one paragraph for each side of the argument.

Complete Kayleigh's answer below. Aim for a Level 4 response.

> The transfiguration defies natural law which is why modern Christians don't find it easy to accept. None of us have ever seen anything like that happen, it sounds like an hallucination. Maybe it wasn't a trick. Mark thinks it happened because Jesus was the Son of God.

Swap your answer with a partner and use the grid on page 24 to mark each other's response. Put a helpful comment at the end of their answer.

WHAT DO YOU THINK?

Improve your skill with the (d) question

The (d) question starts by asking you for your views, then goes further and asks for an opposite view. Remember that you have to consider Christian belief in your answer, so tell the examiner clearly. A good way is to start with *'Some Christians would say…'* or *'Most Christians believe…'* This leaves it open for you to develop your argument and the examiner can be clear that you have covered an important requirement of the question.

Here are some examples of (d) questions from the section you have just studied:

'The idea that Jesus needed to be baptized doesn't make sense.'

'The transfiguration couldn't possibly have happened.'

'Jesus had to be baptized.'

In your answer you should refer to Christianity.

(i) Do you agree? Give reasons for your opinion. (3)

(ii) Give reasons why some people may disagree with you. (3)

Amit decided to respond to the statement, '**The idea that Jesus needed to be baptized doesn't make sense.**' Here is his answer along with the examiner's marks.

(i) Well I don't agree because Jesus wouldn't do anything that didn't make sense. Christians believe that he was the Son of God. ✓ (1 mark for a brief reason) Everything he did was part of God's plan. ✓ (1 mark for a brief reason) By allowing himself to be baptized, Jesus was showing others it was important to repent and be baptized like John the Baptist said. ✓ (3rd mark for a well explained reason)

(ii) You could say it didn't make sense because the Son of God was perfect ✓ (1 mark for a brief reason) and that means Jesus didn't commit any sins that he could repent. ✓ (1 mark for an expanded reason) Some people say how could John, who is only human, forgive someone as important as Jesus. That doesn't make sense either. ✓ (3rd mark for a well explained reason)

Below is the start of Anna's response to the statement, '**The transfiguration couldn't possibly have happened.**' As you can see, she has managed **two** brief reasons in part (i). Complete part (i) to gain another mark, then write an answer to part (ii) to gain the full marks.

(i) I definitely think the transfiguration did happen. This is because Mark reports it in detail and why would he lie. ✓ (1 mark) Just because we have never seen anything like it doesn't make it impossible for God to do… ✓ (1 mark)

The calming of the storm

In this topic you will examine the story of the calming of the storm to see what it shows about Jesus and why it causes problems for Christians today.

nature miracle a miracle in which Jesus shows his power over nature

The background

Mark used this story to show the power Jesus had over nature. In this account, Jesus performed a **nature miracle**.

The storm was so severe that the disciples feared for their lives, despite some of them being experienced fishermen and used to this lake.

Jesus didn't demonstrate any fear.

Jesus spoke directly to the wind and waves and ordered them to stop; they obeyed.

After all his teachings, it seemed Jesus' disciples did not have faith in his ability to keep them from harm.

Jesus' actions shocked the disciples into realizing that he had power over nature.

> " That day when evening came, he said to his disciples, "Let us go over to the other side." Leaving the crowd behind, they took him along, just as he was, in the boat. There were also other boats with him. *A furious squall came up, and the waves broke over the boat, so that it was nearly swamped. Jesus was in the stern, sleeping on a cushion.* The disciples woke him and said to him, "Teacher, don't you care if we drown?"
>
> *He got up, rebuked the wind and said to the waves, "Quiet! Be still!" Then the wind died down and it was completely calm.*
>
> He said to his disciples, *"Why are you so afraid? Do you still have no faith?"*
>
> They were terrified and asked each other, *"Who is this? Even the wind and the waves obey him!"*
>
> (4:35–41) "

What is this story in Mark telling his readers?

Mark used this story to show that Jesus was the Son of God with divine power over nature and the ability to make the elements obey him. It is significant that in the story Jesus spoke directly to the wind and the waves and told them off for their savage behaviour. Many of Mark's early readers would have believed that a storm was caused by the power of evil. Jesus demonstrated his power over evil by commanding the storm to stop.

Some readers notice that the disciples ignored Jesus when all was calm but the minute trouble brewed they panicked and turned to him for help. They had no faith in their own abilities to get out of trouble nor trusted that Jesus would keep them from harm.

Mark was writing at a time when the early Christians were being persecuted for their faith. Perhaps he was using the story to reassure early Christians that God could be relied upon to come to their aid and save them from evil.

This is how a modern artist interpreted the moment in the story when the disciples were nearly swamped by the waters. Compare the horror and fear on their faces with the calm authority shown on the face of Jesus.

What problems does this story cause for Christians today?

Some Christians accept the story as it is told, arguing that all things are possible with God so his Son would have the same power. Others find it difficult to take the story at its face value – someone standing up in a boat and talking to the weather is hardly a convincing start. When it is stated that the weather did as it was told and calmed down, the account begins to sound like a fairytale. For some Christians today, the key to understanding the story is to think of it symbolically:

- The boat = the Christian Church.
- The storm = trouble, such as persecution.

When the people in the boat asked Jesus for help, he came to their aid.

Activity 1

This incident ends with the disciples asking, "Who is this?" but Mark had already given the answer in the story. What is the answer and what is the evidence?

Activity 2

Mark's readers would have known Psalm 89:8–9 which states: "O Lord God Almighty … You rule over the surging sea; when its waves mount up, you still them."

What would this lead the disciples to understand about the identity of Jesus?

Activity 3

Explain why some Christians might say this is a story about faith, whilst others might say it is about good triumphing over evil.

Check you have learnt:

- what happened in the story of the calming of the storm
- what the story could symbolize
- what problems Christians today have with this story.

TRY YOUR SKILL AT THIS

The (b) question:

Do you think the nature miracles are anything more than tricks?

Give **two** reasons for your point of view. (4)

In this topic you will study Mark's account of the feeding of the five thousand and consider what it shows readers about Jesus, then consider the problems this story has for Christians today.

The background

Jesus was already well into his ministry and his disciples had also been out preaching and healing on their own. This miracle happened when the disciples had just met up with Jesus and were telling him about their activities. They were all hungry and needed a rest, but the crowds continued to press around Jesus wanting to hear more.

> So they went away by themselves in a boat to a solitary place. But many who saw them leaving recognised them and ran on foot from all the towns and got there ahead of them. *When Jesus landed and saw a large crowd, he had compassion on them*, **because** *they were like sheep without a shepherd*. So he began teaching them many things.
>
> By this time it was late in the day, so his disciples came to him. "This is a remote place," they said, "and it's already very late. *Send the people away so they can go to the surrounding countryside and villages and buy themselves something to eat.*"
>
> But he answered, "You give them something to eat."
>
> They said to him, "That would take eight months of a man's wages! Are we to go and spend that much on bread and give it to them to eat?"
>
> "How many loaves do you have?" he asked. "Go and see."
>
> When they found out, they said, "Five – and two fish."
>
> Then Jesus directed them to have all the people sit down in groups on the green grass. So they sat down in groups of hundreds and fifties. *Taking the five loaves and the two fish and looking up to heaven, he gave thanks and broke the loaves. Then he gave them to his disciples to set before the people.* He also divided the two fish among them all. They all ate and were satisfied, and the disciples picked up twelve basketfuls of broken pieces of bread and fish. *The number of the men who had eaten was five thousand.*
>
> **(6:32–44)**

Jesus' instinctive feeling was one of compassion for all the people who had made a big effort to follow him.

Sheep without a shepherd are likely to wander off and get lost. This is the same idea as people without a teacher losing their way to God.

The disciples wanted to get rid of the hungry people. Jesus' reaction was to find a way to feed everyone.

Five loaves and two fish were obviously not enough for the crowd.

Jesus' behaviour was very significant. He looked to God, gave thanks, broke the bread and shared it with everyone. The Last Supper was foreshadowed here.

Mark's account is specific about the large number that was fed that day.

Stories like the feeding of the five thousand teach Christians the importance of sharing what they have with others.

This modern painting of the miracle shows the crowd enjoying a day out in the park and sharing fish and chips. You can partially see Jesus in the top right-hand corner as the priest, who has finished celebrating the Eucharist and is reading the parish notices. What do you think the artist is saying when she shows some people listening intently and others turning their backs and concentrating on their food?

Activity 1

Draw a Venn diagram to show the similarities and differences between this story and the calming of the storm on page 108.

Activity 2

Explain the following key elements of the story:

- compassion
- power over nature
- the Last Supper.

What does Mark's account tell readers about Jesus?

Mark's account shows how Jesus felt compassion for the people who had followed him. They showed faith in him and he rewarded them. Although the disciples wanted to get rid of the crowd, Jesus took responsibility for feeding them. The miraculous element of this story, which shows that Jesus had power over nature, also tells the reader that God can make all things possible. Just as in the calming of the storm, those who turn to Jesus for help receive it.

Readers of Mark's Gospel would recognize Jesus' actions as a forerunner of the Last Supper where Jesus gave thanks for the bread, broke it and then shared it with his followers. Others might understand that this event fulfilled Old Testament prophecies of a Messiah who would come and feed his people like Moses fed the people in the wilderness.

What problems does this story cause for Christians today?

Once again, it is the difficulty of believing in the impossible. Everyone knows you can't produce food from nothing.

Some Christians do believe the story is literally true because God is powerful enough to make anything happen. Others suggest that what really happened was that Jesus set an example by sharing the small amount of food he had brought with him and others then copied. This led to everyone having something to eat. It is also possible that Mark exaggerated the size of the crowd.

Many modern Christians think that Mark never intended his readers to take the story at face value, so they look for a deeper meaning. They believe Jesus was showing his followers that it was their duty to help the poor and feed the hungry. The problem is that no matter how much people undertake this responsibility, there are always hungry people.

✓ Check you have learnt:

- what happened in the story of the feeding of the five thousand
- what explanations there could be for this miracle
- what problems Christians today have with the story.

TRY YOUR SKILL AT THIS

The (d) question:

'It is impossible to believe in miracles today.'

In your answer you should refer to Christianity.

(i) Do you agree? Give reasons for your opinion. (3)

(ii) Give reasons why some people may disagree with you. (3)

Jesus walks on water

In this topic you will study the story of Jesus walking on the lake and consider what it meant for Mark, and why it might cause problems for some Christians today.

The background

This account follows immediately after the feeding of the five thousand, when the crowd was astonished by Jesus' ability to perform miracles. Jesus did not want celebrity status, or to draw the attention of the authorities to him as a rabble rouser. He began to move away to quiet and solitude.

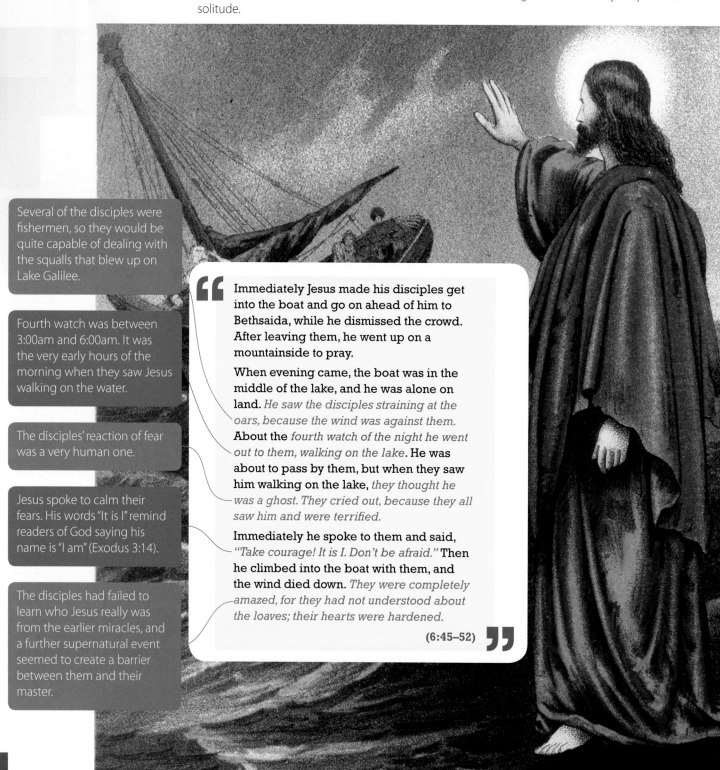

Several of the disciples were fishermen, so they would be quite capable of dealing with the squalls that blew up on Lake Galilee.

Fourth watch was between 3:00am and 6:00am. It was the very early hours of the morning when they saw Jesus walking on the water.

The disciples' reaction of fear was a very human one.

Jesus spoke to calm their fears. His words "It is I" remind readers of God saying his name is "I am" (Exodus 3:14).

The disciples had failed to learn who Jesus really was from the earlier miracles, and a further supernatural event seemed to create a barrier between them and their master.

> " Immediately Jesus made his disciples get into the boat and go on ahead of him to Bethsaida, while he dismissed the crowd. After leaving them, he went up on a mountainside to pray.
>
> When evening came, the boat was in the middle of the lake, and he was alone on land. *He saw the disciples straining at the oars, because the wind was against them.* About the *fourth watch of the night he went out to them, walking on the lake.* He was about to pass by them, but when they saw him walking on the lake, *they thought he was a ghost. They cried out, because they all saw him and were terrified.*
>
> Immediately he spoke to them and said, *"Take courage! It is I. Don't be afraid."* Then he climbed into the boat with them, and the wind died down. *They were completely amazed, for they had not understood about the loaves; their hearts were hardened.*
>
> **(6:45–52)** "

What did Mark understand from this incident?

Mark's Gospel has already told a story about Jesus having power over the sea (see page 108) and both stories share symbolic features. The sea with its fierce waves represents evil, and Jesus with his calming words represents good overcoming evil.

Many of Mark's readers would also recognize Jesus' actions as the fulfilment of Old Testament prophecies about the Messiah. Psalm 77:19 states: 'Your path led through sea, your way through the mighty waters, though your footprints were not seen.' When Jesus told the terrified disciples, "It is I" they recognized those words as the ones God used when he spoke to Moses from the burning bush. All of this built up the picture that Jesus was the Messiah, the Son of God. Only someone with divine power could conquer the waves.

What problems does this story cause for Christians today?

Nobody can walk on water. This sort of feat goes against the laws of nature and modern Christians either have to accept Mark's account literally or consider it as a story with meaning.

Walking on water appears to go against the laws of nature, but one animal can perform this feat. The Basiliscus lizard is also called the 'Jesus Lizard' because it can run along the surface of the water. Flaps on its feet trap the air, enabling it to move over water.

Did he? Didn't he?

Those Christians who accept that Jesus walked on water argue that God is all-powerful and the Bible contains the words of God. They say it must have happened like that because there is no other explanation for a person walking on water. In their view, Jesus chose to miraculously walk on water to show the disciples he was the Son of God who had power over nature. Mark's account states that the disciples had not understood the feeding of the five thousand, so perhaps Jesus was trying to teach them again by using a different example.

Some people have suggested that Jesus only appeared to walk on water. This event took place in the early hours of the morning. The disciples would have been tired and perhaps not seeing clearly. Mists often sit over water and make things look strange; in fact, the disciples thought they were seeing a ghost. It is also possible that Jesus was standing on a sandbank and appeared to be walking on water.

Some point out that the story has so many symbolic elements, which show it was never intended to be taken literally. They believe that Mark told this story as an example of the power of good; Jesus was good and he had power over evil in the form of the storm. Mark was writing at a time of great persecution for early Christians, so his story would have given them comfort. It shows Jesus coming to the aid of his followers before they even asked for help. It also shows that Jesus was strong enough to save them.

Another argument against taking the story literally is that it contains two Old Testament references that Mark's readers would understand to mean Jesus was the Messiah who was foretold.

Activity 1

Role play a Sunday television chat show discussion between two modern Christians who disagree in their interpretation of the walking on water story.

Activity 2

Explain the common beliefs about Jesus that are shown in the walking on water story and the calming of the storm story (see page 108).

Activity 3

a) Using the material here, draw two columns on your page and note down the arguments for and against Jesus walking on water.

b) What do you think this story is about and why?

✓ **Check you have learnt:**

- what happened in the story of Jesus walking on water
- what deeper meaning the story could have
- why this account might cause problems for Christians today.

TRY YOUR SKILL AT THIS

The (c) question:

Explain why the account of Jesus walking on the water causes problems for some Christians today. (8)

In this topic you will study the healing of Legion and learn what Mark's account shows readers about Jesus, and then consider why this story causes problems for some Christians.

KEYWORDS KEYWORDS

Legion a man from whom Jesus cast out many demons

healing miracle a miracle in which Jesus shows his power over sickness

The background

Jesus had crossed Lake Galilee into an area called Gerasenes, which was a non-Jewish (Gentile) country. People kept pigs for food there, but in the Jewish area such animals were forbidden in the scriptures because they were considered unclean.

> They went across the lake to the region of the Gerasenes. When Jesus got out of the boat, a man with an evil spirit came from the tombs to meet him. *This man lived in the tombs, and no one could bind him any more, not even with a chain. For he had often been chained hand and foot, but he tore the chains apart and broke the irons on his feet. No one was strong enough to subdue him.* Night and day among the tombs and in the hills he would cry out and cut himself with stones.
>
> When he saw Jesus from a distance, he ran and fell on his knees in front of him. He shouted at the top of his voice, *"What do you want with me, Jesus, Son of the Most High God? Swear to God that you won't torture me!"* For Jesus had said to him, "Come out of this man, you evil spirit!"
>
> Then Jesus asked him, "What is your name?"
>
> *"My name is Legion,"* he replied, *"for we are many."* And he begged Jesus again and again not to send them out of the area.
>
> A large herd of pigs was feeding on the nearby hillside. The demons begged Jesus, "Send us among the pigs; allow us to go into them." He gave them permission, and the evil spirits came out and went into the pigs. The herd, about two thousand in number, rushed down the steep bank into the lake and were drowned.
>
> Those tending the pigs ran off and reported this in the town and countryside, and the people went out to see what had happened. When they came to Jesus, they saw the man who had been possessed by the legion of demons, sitting there, dressed and in his right mind; and they were afraid. Those who had seen it told the people what had happened to the demon-possessed man – and told about the pigs as well. *Then the people began to plead with Jesus to leave their region.*
>
> As Jesus was getting into the boat, the man who had been demon-possessed begged to go with him. Jesus did not let him, but said, *"Go home to your family and tell them how much the Lord has done for you, and how he has had mercy on you."* So the man went away and began to tell in the Decapolis how much Jesus had done for him. And all the people were amazed.
>
> (5:1–20)

The man lived amongst tombs, which were usually caves. The strength of his madness was shown by the chains used to hold him down and stop him self-harming.

The man recognized who Jesus was without being told; or it may have been the evil spirits speaking. The evil spirits knew who Jesus was and feared his power.

This probably meant that the man was possessed by thousands of devils.

Jesus' power was so great that it frightened people.

Although Jesus did not usually want his miracles spoken about at home in Jewish occupied territory for fear of upsetting the authorities, here he permitted his message to be given to the Gentiles.

What was Mark saying in this account?

This story shows Mark's readers that Jesus had power over evil. This is another miracle story. It was a **healing miracle** because the man was cured of his madness. It can also be thought of as a nature miracle because Jesus exerted his power over the forces of evil that possessed the man.

As you have discovered in previous stories, Mark's accounts frequently contain symbolic elements. The man possessed by spirits lived in a world of darkness amongst the cave tombs. The powers of evil held him tightly in their power, as the description of the iron chains shows. Once the man was healed by Jesus, he lost his chains and came out into the light.

What is also significant is that the man, or the spirits that possessed him, instantly recognized Jesus as the Son of God, and that recognition frightened the spirits. They knew how powerful Jesus was. Appropriately, the evil spirits were exorcised into pigs, which Jewish scriptures state are unclean animals.

The name the man gave made no real sense. 'Legion' was not a person's name but the name for a contingent of 6000 Roman soldiers. The reason the man gave for his name was "for we are many", perhaps suggesting that he was possessed by 6000 demons, which would be a serious attack of evil.

Why does this story cause problems for some Christians?

Some modern Christians have no problems with the story. For them, Mark wrote a precise account of events that happened.

For other Christians, this story seems to be about exorcism and evil spirits, which has little to do with life in the twenty-first century. They recognize that the man was suffering from a mental disorder that made him self-harm. Ideas about demons being cast into pigs belong to ancient superstitions. Some Christians have suggested that it was the screams and cries of the man as he went into a fit that actually spooked the herd of pigs: they panicked and raced off over the hillside to their death. The pig herdsmen, who should have been looking after the animals, had been too busy watching Jesus. Knowing they would be in trouble for losing the herd, the men told their master a story of demons and supernatural forces.

Not only does Mark's story seem improbable to modern Christians, it also suggests that Jesus was quite prepared to send 2000 animals to a cruel death. This doesn't fit in with most Christians' belief that Jesus was compassionate to all living creatures.

Some have interpreted the death of the pigs as showing that Jesus would do anything to help a person escape the clutches of evil and that a human life is always worth more than an animal's.

Activity 1

Do you think it matters to modern Christians if the story did not happen exactly as Mark described it? Give **two** reasons to support your opinion.

Activity 2

Write Legion's blog giving his view of what happened. Describe the way his neighbours behaved towards him before and after the healing.

Activity 3

What further information does this gospel story give about the identity of Jesus?

✓ **Check you have learnt:**

- the events in the story of Legion
- what interpretations of the story are possible
- why some Christians today have problems with the account.

TRY YOUR SKILL AT THIS

The (b) question:

Do you think the story of Legion has anything to teach Christians today?

Give **two** reasons for your point of view. (4)

The raising of Jairus' daughter

In this topic you will examine the raising of Jairus' daughter and consider what Mark's account shows about Jesus, and then consider what problems it causes for some Christians today.

The background

The story of **Jairus**' daughter is written in two halves – a 'before' and an 'after' scene. Sandwiched in the middle is another story about Jesus' healing powers. The two healing stories are linked by the common theme of faith. The people involved received healing because they believed Jesus had that power. It was their faith in God, rather than the words or actions of Jesus, that made the people whole again.

> When Jesus had again crossed over by boat to the other side of the lake, a large crowd gathered around him while he was by the lake. Then *one of the synagogue rulers, named Jairus, came there. Seeing Jesus, he fell at his feet and pleaded earnestly with him,* "My little daughter is dying. Please come and put your hands on her so that she will be healed and live." So Jesus went with him.
>
> A large crowd followed and pressed around him. And a woman was there who had been subject to bleeding for twelve years. She had suffered a great deal under the care of many doctors and had spent all she had, yet instead of getting better she grew worse. When she heard about Jesus, she came up behind him in the crowd and touched his cloak, because she thought, *"If I just touch his clothes, I will be healed."* Immediately her bleeding stopped and she felt in her body that she was freed from her suffering.
>
> At once Jesus realized that power had gone out from him. He turned around in the crowd and asked, "Who touched my clothes?"
>
> "You see the people crowding against you," his disciples answered, "and yet you can ask, 'Who touched me?'"
>
> But Jesus kept looking around to see who had done it. Then the woman, knowing what had happened to her, came and fell at his feet and, trembling with fear, told him the whole truth. He said to her, *"Daughter, your faith has healed you. Go in peace and be freed from your suffering."*
>
> While Jesus was still speaking, some men came from the house of Jairus, the synagogue ruler. "Your daughter is dead," they said. "Why bother the teacher any more?"
>
> Ignoring what they said, Jesus told the synagogue ruler, *"Don't be afraid; just believe."*
>
> He did not let anyone follow him except Peter, James and John the brother of James. When they came to the home of the synagogue ruler, Jesus saw a commotion, with people crying and wailing loudly. He went in and said to them, "Why all this commotion and wailing? *The child is not dead but asleep."* But they laughed at him.
>
> *After he put them all out, he took the child's father and mother and the disciples who were with him, and went in where the child was.* He took her by the hand and said to her, *"Talitha koum!"* (which means, "Little girl, I say to you, get up!"). *Immediately the girl stood up and walked around* (she was twelve years old). At this they were completely astonished. *He gave strict orders not to let anyone know about this, and told them to give her something to eat.*
>
> (5:21–43)

As a synagogue ruler, Jairus was important in the religious community, yet he got down on his knees to ask Jesus for his help. Jairus had faith that Jesus could heal his daughter.

The woman had faith that even the smallest contact with Jesus would be sufficient to cure her.

Jesus said it was her faith in God, not touching his clothes, which healed her. He called her "daughter" linking her to God the Father. She confessed fully what she had done and Jesus sent her away in peace. Faith in God had restored her body to full health.

This teaching that faith in God is what matters, sums up both stories.

This could mean that Jesus knew the girl was just unconscious and not dead, or it could mean that death is like sleep until God resurrects people.

Jesus needed no audience; he took his three closest disciples and the girl's parents.

Jesus' words are written in Aramaic, which he would have spoken. This suggests this may well be an eyewitness account of the incident. The girl responded to Jesus' command and got up and walked.

Jesus did not seek publicity. Very practically, he suggested the girl needed food after her ordeal.

What does Mark show in these stories?

Although appearing to be just two accounts of Jesus healing people, Mark gave them several layers of deeper meaning. It is significant that Jesus healed females, who would have been less important than men in Jewish society at that time. The woman with the bleeding disorder would have been on the margin of society because anyone touching her would become ritually unclean. The other was only a child, albeit the daughter of a high-ranking Jewish religious leader, so she would not have been important in society. Jesus' healing of both shows that everyone is included in his ministry.

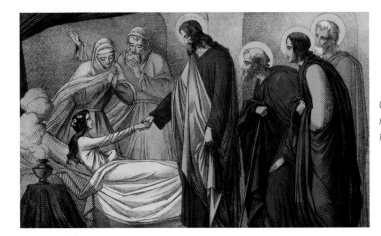

One artist's idea of Jesus raising Jairus' daughter from the dead.

These accounts show that Jesus had power over life and death. The woman with the bleeding was weakened by her long-standing illness; after contact with Jesus her body was made whole again.

The daughter of Jairus was dead. Although Jesus said she was just sleeping, the people at Jairus' house were sure she was dead. This was more than a healing miracle; it showed Jesus had power over death. Some scholars have suggested that by showing that Jesus had power over life and death, Mark was pointing his readers towards Jesus' resurrection.

Mark used both accounts to show that people who had faith in Jesus as the Son of God would be rewarded for that faith. The woman did not feel the need to approach Jesus formally, possibly because her illness was embarrassing. Or perhaps she did not want to compromise Jesus' purity through contact with her. Her faith was such that she believed even the minimum of contact would work miracles for her.

Jairus was more surprising because, as a synagogue leader, he would have encountered a lot of prejudice against this teacher from Nazareth who did not keep the rules. Jairus must have been very convinced by Jesus to go down on his knees before him in public and declare faith in Jesus' healing powers.

For Mark, both stories showed how Jesus had the power to turn despair into hope. In the case of Jairus' daughter, Mark was also telling his readers that death is not the end for those with faith in Jesus.

What problems might this story cause for Christians today?

All miracle stories cause difficulties for Christians today because miracles do not seem to happen in the modern world, and people don't come back from the dead. This means that Christians have to either accept the story at face value, because Jesus was divine and could do things an ordinary mortal could not, or look for another explanation.

Mark's stories often point to deeper truths about Jesus' identity, so some Christians today are not concerned whether the events really happened as Mark described. What matters more is the message behind those stories about faith.

Others think Jairus' daughter was really in a coma, or perhaps deeply asleep as Jesus said. This would explain why she awoke and was soon walking around. If she really was dead, then some Christians wonder why Jesus used his powers over death to raise only her and a few others.

KEYWORDS KEYWORD

Jairus the synagogue ruler whose daughter was brought back to life by Jesus

Activity 1

Explain how both healing stories in this account show the importance of having faith.

Activity 2

Create a mind-map of this gospel story to display the different interpretations.

Activity 3

Why could the story of Jairus' daughter lead Mark's readers towards Jesus' resurrection?

✓ **Check you have learnt:**

- what happened in the story of Jairus' daughter
- what Mark said this showed about Jesus
- why this account causes problems for some Christians today.

TRY YOUR SKILL AT THIS

The (d) question:

'Raising Jairus' daughter from the dead defies belief.'

In your answer you should refer to Christianity.

(i) Do you agree? Give reasons for your opinion. (3)

(ii) Give reasons why some people may disagree with you. (3)

SKILLS COACHING 11

DO YOU KNOW?

Improve your skill with the (a) question

Can you identify the correct **KEYWORD** from Chapter 4 to match the definitions?

> ? = a man from whom Jesus cast out many demons

> ? = a miracle in which Jesus shows his power over nature

> ? = the synagogue ruler whose daughter was brought back to life by Jesus

> ? = a miracle in which Jesus shows his power over sickness

Improve your skill with the (c) question

Many of the (c) questions for this chapter will be concerned with how modern Christians understand accounts in Mark's Gospel. This is especially interesting when you are dealing with miracle stories which seem, at first, to be very difficult for modern Christians to understand. Make sure that you have learnt the symbolic elements within each story because many Christians today think that was what Mark was directing his readers to do. But don't forget as well that some Christians today do accept the miracles as literal accounts of what happened.

A typical (c) question about the material you have just studied will ask you to '**Explain why** [one of the miracles] **causes problems for Christians today.**'

The question assumes that there will be problems, so don't bother to tell the examiner why some Christians think the account is fine. That will not get you any marks. You need to think about reasons why the supernatural happenings don't fit into twenty-first-century living. Also consider whether Jesus' actions go against twenty-first-century attitudes, for example, sending thousands of animals over a cliff to their death.

Here is one question you could try out this approach on:

> **Explain why the healing of Legion causes problems for some Christians today.** (8)

Can you think of any other questions that you might be asked in this section?

Plan an answer for the question above, or one of your own devising. Use the step-by-step approach and aim for **two** examples with expanded reasons. Keep the plan handy for revision.

● One brief reason. ● Not explaining but describing the issue.	1–2 marks
● Two brief reasons. ● One expanded reason.	3–4 marks
● Three brief reasons. ● One fully developed reason. ● Two reasons with one expanded.	5–6 marks
● Four brief reasons. ● Two expanded reasons. ● Three reasons with one expanded.	7–8 marks

WHAT DO YOU THINK?

Improve your skill with the (b) question

Try out your skills on this (b) question:

> Do you think Jesus did raise Jairus' daughter from the dead?
>
> Give **two** reasons for your point of view. (4)

Remember the step-by-step approach?

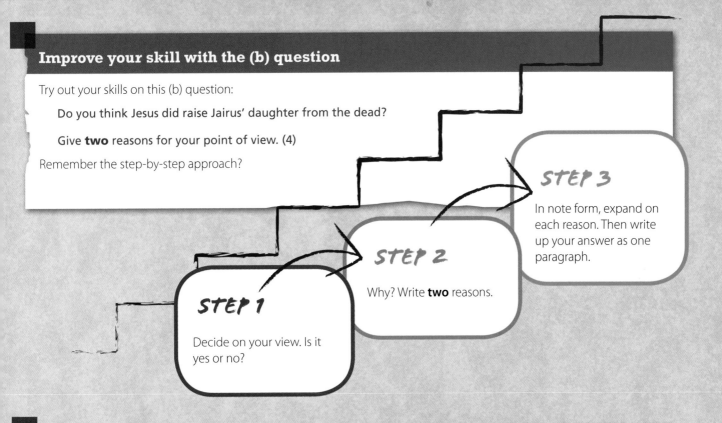

STEP 1

Decide on your view. Is it yes or no?

STEP 2

Why? Write **two** reasons.

STEP 3

In note form, expand on each reason. Then write up your answer as one paragraph.

Improve your skill with the (d) question

Remember to use a similar approach for the (d) question. Once you have planned out your view, do the same for the opposite view and make this a separate paragraph.

Try this (d) question:

> 'Healing miracles are easier for modern Christians to accept than miracles over nature.'
>
> In your answer you should refer to Christianity.
>
> (i) Do you agree? Give reasons for your opinion. (3)
>
> (ii) Give reasons why some people may disagree with you. (3)

! A tip:
Have you remembered to link your answer to Christianity?

What does 'Messiah' mean?

In this topic you will look at the meaning of the title 'Messiah' and consider its significance for Christians today.

The background

As you have learnt during your study of Mark's Gospel, the writer was concerned with showing his readers that Jesus was the Messiah who was promised in the Old Testament. We have referred to this many times in this book, so it is useful to draw all the evidence together now to understand the full picture.

What does the word 'Messiah' mean?

'Messiah' is the Hebrew word for 'the anointed one'. When the word is translated into Greek it becomes 'Christ', which is the name most often used with Jesus' name; Jesus Christ means Jesus the anointed one. It is a tradition in many cultures that the person who becomes king or queen is anointed. In Judaism, a small amount of sweet-smelling oil was ceremonially smeared on the head of a new king or a priest. It was a sign to everyone present that this person's power was recognized by God.

What did the Jews think the Messiah would do?

The Old Testament, the holy book of the Jews, contains many references to a Messiah who will come and save the Jews.

The scriptures state that the Messiah would be a descendant of the great Jewish leader of a thousand years earlier, King David, but be even more powerful than David. The Messiah would be the one to save the Jews from evil.

Different groups of Jews interpreted these references in their own way but all agreed a Messiah would come in the future to save them. Only a few expected the Messiah would come in their lifetime, most thought God would send the Messiah at the end of time. The scriptures state that they would know when the Messiah was on his way because the prophet Elijah would return to earth to herald the Messiah's arrival. The Jews believed the Messiah would destroy the evil that threatened them and establish a new kingdom. Some interpreted this to mean the Messiah would end the Roman occupation of their land and set up a new kingdom with a new ruler. Others thought the Messianic age, the name given to the rule of the Messiah, would be a spiritual time of peace.

Activity 1

Explain the ideas about Jesus as the Messiah that appear in the line of this hymn:

"Hail to the Lord's anointed, great David's greater son!"

What did Mark say the Messiah would do?

As you will remember from your studies throughout this book, the disciples had great difficulty understanding what sort of Messiah Jesus was. Mark's Gospel shows Jesus trying to teach them that the Messiah would save them from evil and death and that the new kingdom he was establishing was God's kingdom.

You have studied several stories where Jesus did something amazing, which marked him out as the Messiah, but Jesus asked those who had witnessed the event to keep it secret. This was because Jesus knew how dangerous the idea of a Messiah could be when people misunderstood it. If the Romans had believed that Jesus was the Messiah who some of the Jews were expecting, then they would have had him executed immediately, as a military threat.

Throughout his gospel, Mark showed his readers that Jesus was the Messiah foretold in the scriptures. Many of Mark's stories incorporate words or ideas that echo specific prophecies about the Messiah. Jesus was a descendant of King David, although Mark did not write a nativity account to prove this. Mark wanted his readers to understand that the Messiah came to save his followers from sin. To do this, Jesus had to pay the price for those sins by giving his life and then rising from the dead to show that sin had been overcome. Both he and his followers would then have eternal life.

For Mark, it was essential to show his readers that Jesus predicted his death and resurrection. Both are vital if Mark's readers are to be guided away from the idea that Jesus was a failure and executed as a criminal.

What do Christians today think about the Messiah concept?

Although the Messiah concept belongs to Judaism, it is still important to modern Christians. Their understanding of Jesus as the Messiah is of a leader to guide them through life and lead them away from sin and death. Some might use the term 'Messiah' and others might choose the Greek word 'Christ' to show their belief that Jesus was the one promised by God.

Christians believe that their faith in Jesus as the Messiah, the Christ, means God will grant them forgiveness for their sins and give them life after death.

The idea of the Messiah as the suffering servant (see page 122 for more detail) has inspired many Christians through the ages to follow in Jesus' footsteps in a humble way, rejecting violence.

Christians, past and present, have to believe in the concept of the Messiah otherwise, in the words of St Paul, 'their faith would be in vain'. If Jesus was not the Messiah, then everything would be a sham. Many events in Jesus' lifetime, and after his resurrection, have convinced Christians that Jesus was the anointed Son of God, the Messiah.

> "Who do you say I am?"
> Peter answered, "You are the Christ."
>
> (8:29)

> "Let's see if Elijah comes to take him down,"
> he said.
>
> (15:36)

> "Are you the Christ, the Son of the Blessed One?"
> "I am," said Jesus.
>
> (14:61–62)

> "Hosanna! Blessed is he who comes in the name of the Lord!
> Blessed is the coming kingdom of our father David!"
>
> (11:9–10)

Activity 2

Draw a Venn diagram. Label the left circle JEWISH IDEA, the right circle JESUS and the overlapping section in the centre MESSIAH. In the appropriate section, write the ideas you have learnt on these pages and elsewhere in this book.

Activity 3

Copy out each of these quotations from passages in Mark that you have studied. Explain how each links to the Messiah concept.

✓ **Check you have learnt:**

- the sort of Messiah the Jews expected
- the sort of Messiah Mark said Jesus was
- how Christians today interpret the concept of the Messiah.

TRY YOUR SKILL AT THIS

The (d) question:

'Jesus as the Messiah must have been a big disappointment to the Jews.'

In your answer you should refer to Christianity.

(i) Do you agree? Give reasons for your opinion. (3)

(ii) Give reasons why some people may disagree with you. (3)

In this topic you will examine the title 'Son of Man' and consider what it shows about Jesus and its significance for Christians today.

KEYWORDS KEYWORD

Son of Man a title used by Jesus of himself, probably meaning he would suffer before bringing in God's kingdom

Useful specialist language

parousia the belief that Jesus will return at the end of time to judge everyone

The background

You may have noticed in the passages you have studied that when Jesus referred to himself, the title he most frequently used was '**Son of Man**'. As you saw on page 80, it was only at his trial that Jesus acknowledged he was the Messiah and he rarely called himself the Son of God. 'Son of Man' was the title Jesus preferred but no one else called him by that name. For those reasons, it is important to understand what Jesus meant by the title and its significance.

Christians have put forward various reasons why Jesus preferred the title 'Son of Man' and what he meant by it. At one level, it stressed his humanity because every man can accurately describe himself as a son of man, as every woman could call herself a daughter of man. Others believe the title was useful because it would not have interested the Roman authorities.

The Son of Man in the Old Testament

The title 'Son of Man' would have been familiar to Jesus, his followers and many readers of Mark's Gospel because it appeared in Old Testament scriptures in the Book of Daniel.

1. The authority of God

The Book of Daniel states:

> In my vision at night I looked, and there before me was one like a son of man, coming with the clouds of heaven. He approached the Ancient of Days and was led into his presence. He was given authority, glory and sovereign power; all peoples, nations and men of every language worshipped him. His dominion is an everlasting dominion that will not pass away, and his kingdom is one that will never be destroyed.
>
> **(Daniel 7:13–14)**

In a dream, Daniel sees an old man sitting in judgement who gives the 'Son of Man' the power to act. Reference to this story would help Jesus' followers to understand who he was and why he could achieve miraculous things that no ordinary human was capable of. This title gave Jesus God's authority to forgive sins and break religious rules on earth.

2. Suffering servant

Other references to the Son of Man in the Old Testament show him accepting punishment for crimes he did not commit in order to spare others. In the Book of Isaiah, the Son of Man is a suffering servant:

> He was despised and rejected by men, a man of sorrows, and familiar with suffering. ... But he was pierced for our transgressions [mistakes], he was crushed for our iniquities [wrongdoings]; the punishment that brought us peace was upon him, and by his wounds we are healed.
>
> **(Isaiah 53:3 and 5)**

By using the title 'Son of Man', Jesus linked himself to the servant in Isaiah. This showed his was a totally different mission to that of the political Messiah most Jews expected. In Mark's Gospel, Jesus told them: "For even the Son of Man did not come to be served, but to serve, and to give his life as a ransom for many." (10:45).

Activity 1

Look back to page 80 and compare Jesus' words to the High Priest with those in Daniel's dream. Explain what the High Priest might have understood Jesus to be saying about his identity.

3. Jesus will return again

On three occasions when Jesus used the title 'Son of Man' he told his disciples that he would return again in judgement at the end of time. This belief that Jesus will come to earth a second time is called the parousia.

Many Christians believe that Jesus' words to the High Priest at the trial show this:

> And you will see the Son of Man sitting at the right hand of the Mighty One and coming on the clouds of heaven.
>
> (14:62)

The artist shows Jesus as the suffering servant.

Jesus used the title 'Son of Man' in Mark's Gospel to mean:

● he had God's authority to forgive sins and overrule Sabbath laws

● he must suffer and die at the hands of sinful men to free people from sin

● he will rise from the dead to give Christians the hope of eternal life

● he will be seen in all his power and glory at the end of the world.

Jan Mostaert, *Christ Crowned With Thorns*, presented by Henry Wagner 1924, © Copyright The National Gallery 2010

Activity 2

Look back to the prophecies Jesus made about his death on pages 30, 70 and 102. Which references to Isaiah's Son of Man are being referred to?

Activity 3

Compare the words of Jesus at his trial (see page 80) with those in Mark 13:26–7 and Mark 8:38. (You will need a Bible or access to an online Bible.) What is Jesus saying the Son of Man is going to do?

Check you have learnt:

● four things Jesus meant by the title 'Son of Man'

● two ways the title was used in the Old Testament

● the significance of the title for Christians today.

TRY YOUR SKILL AT THIS

The (c) question:

Explain why the title 'Son of Man' is significant for Christians today. (8)

What is the significance of the title 'Son of Man' for Christians today?

This title is not one that Christians today use much, which may seem odd because it appears 14 times in Mark's Gospel and was the one Jesus favoured. For most Christians today, the title emphasizes Jesus' humanity. This gives them comfort that Jesus understands the problems they might be going through.

For others, the title shows that Jesus has authority to forgive their sins. In the past, references to the suffering servant have given Christians facing persecution hope and strength. Jesus was the supreme example of how to deal with suffering and carry out the will of God. The 'Son of Man' title also helps Christians to understand the price Jesus paid, on their behalf, so they can enjoy eternal life with God.

The idea that the Son of Man will return at the end of time is a difficult one for modern Christians. In the Creed, they recite their belief that Jesus 'will come again to judge both the living and the dead', which many interpret to mean Jesus will judge their actions when they die.

Jesus as the Son of God

> In this topic you will think about the reasons why reading Mark's Gospel leads some people to believe that Jesus was the Son of God.

The background

The title 'Son of God' is the one most Christians use when talking of Jesus. This is probably because it is more straightforward than Son of Man. There is only one Son of God and the title contains all the ideas of God's power within it. Jesus himself hardly ever used the title, though he never denied it when others used it. It is possible that Jesus didn't use this title because it would play into the hands of the High Priests, who were looking for any opportunity to charge Jesus with blasphemy.

The importance of the title 'Son of God'

As with the other titles discussed on pages 120–121 and 122–123, 'Son of God' was a title that appeared in Jewish scriptures. Readers of Mark's Gospel would have known this and would have been familiar with passages like these:

> When Israel was a child, I loved him, and out of Egypt I called my son.
>
> **(Hosea 11:1)**

> I will proclaim the decree of the Lord: He said to me, "You are my Son; today I have become your Father."
>
> **(Psalm 2:7)**

Both passages focus on the close relationship God the Father had with his Son.

The evidence for Jesus as the Son of God

Mark was so convinced of Jesus' identity that he based the whole Gospel around it. His accounts were designed to show readers that Jesus was the Son of God and, therefore, the Messiah foretold in scriptures. Mark stated his belief in his opening sentence when he wrote: 'The beginning of the gospel about Jesus Christ, the Son of God' (1:1).

After presenting all his evidence in the form of accounts of Jesus' ministry, Mark agreed with the centurion at the foot of the cross (see page 84): "Surely this man was the Son of God!" (15:39).

Mark's Gospel tells Christians that because Jesus was the Son of God he had to suffer. Explain the reason for this. (The word 'ransom' might jog your memory.)

When Jesus was baptized by John, the voice of God was heard (see page 100). God said, "You are my Son, whom I love; with you I am well pleased."

What does the title 'Son of God' tell Christians?

- When God spoke of Jesus at his baptism and transfiguration it was with great love. This shows Christians the closeness that existed between God and Jesus. Many Christians find it easiest to understand this bond as like that between a father and son.

- A son owes it to his father to obey him. This helps Christians to understand Jesus' words in the Garden of Gethsemane (see page 74) and from the cross (see page 84).

- Jesus had to be divine. It was proved through the miracles he performed and his resurrection from the dead. Only the Son of God could do those things, no mere human.

The Son of God for Christians today

This is the title most Christians use today because they recognize Jesus' relationship to God. The concept is an important part of the Creed. If Jesus was not the Son of God, there would be no Christian religion. However, the evidence in Mark's Gospel, supported by many Christians' personal experiences of God, convinces them of the truth of this title.

Christians recite the following words in the Creed. This shows that Jesus as the Son of God is an essential Christian belief.

We believe in one Lord, Jesus Christ, the only Son of God, eternally begotten of the Father, God from God, Light from Light, true God from true God, begotten, not made, of one Being with the Father.

END OF CHAPTER 4 CHECK

✓ Check the (a) question

In this chapter about *The identity of Jesus* you learnt these **KEYWORD**:

| baptism | confession | Elijah | healing miracle | Jairus | John the Baptist |

| Legion | Messiah | Moses | nature miracle | Son of Man | transfiguration |

a) Write three sentences, each using one of the keywords from the list above, to show you understand the meaning of three key terms.

b) Work with a partner to test each other on the meaning of the keywords in this chapter.

✓ Check the (c) question

We have looked at the different ways Jesus showed his followers who he really was:

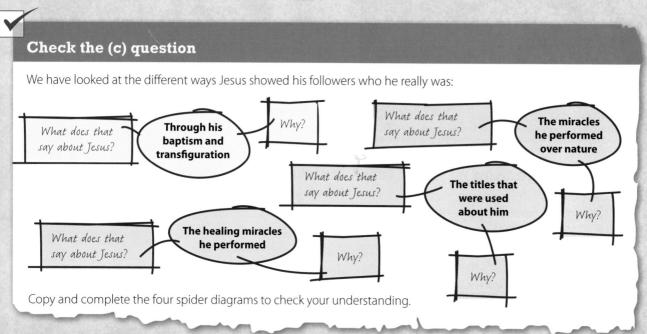

What does that say about Jesus? — **Through his baptism and transfiguration** — Why?

What does that say about Jesus? — **The miracles he performed over nature**

What does that say about Jesus? — **The titles that were used about him** — Why?

What does that say about Jesus? — **The healing miracles he performed** — Why?

Why?

Copy and complete the four spider diagrams to check your understanding.

✓ Check the (b) and (d) questions

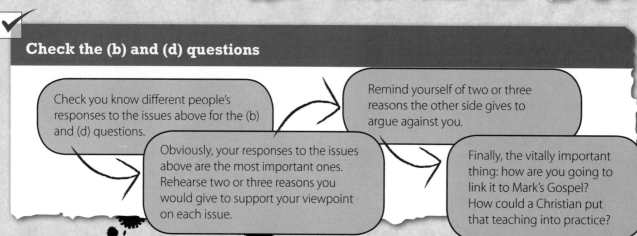

Check you know different people's responses to the issues above for the (b) and (d) questions.

Remind yourself of two or three reasons the other side gives to argue against you.

Obviously, your responses to the issues above are the most important ones. Rehearse two or three reasons you would give to support your viewpoint on each issue.

Finally, the vitally important thing: how are you going to link it to Mark's Gospel? How could a Christian put that teaching into practice?

Here is a typical example of how questions about *The identity of Jesus* might be presented on the exam paper. Choose one of these questions to work through in exam conditions in order to check your progress.

Before the exam, remember to:
- ☑ learn the correct definitions for all keywords
- ☑ revise thoroughly all you need to know. You can use Skills Coaching sections 3, 6, 9 and 12 to help you
- ☑ keep practising the understanding and evaluative skills you have learnt.

SECTION 4 – THE IDENTITY OF JESUS
You must answer ONE question from this section.

EITHER

7 (a) Who was **Elijah**? (2)

   (b) Do you think Jesus' baptism shows that he was sinful?
     Give **two** reasons for your point of view. (4)

   (c) Explain why the title Son of Man is significant for Christians today. (8)

   (d) 'Modern Christians struggle to understand Jesus' miracles.'
     In your answer you should refer to Christianity.
     (i) Do you agree? Give reasons for your opinion. (3)
     (ii) Give reasons why some people may disagree with you. (3)

                  (Total for Question 7 = 20 marks)

OR

8 (a) What does **Son of Man** mean? (2)

   (b) Do you think any of the disciples really knew who Jesus was?
     Give **two** reasons for your point of view. (4)

   (c) Explain why the healing of Legion causes problems for Christians today. (8)

   (d) 'If people at the time didn't recognize who Jesus was, those in the twenty-first century stand no chance.'
     In your answer you should refer to Christianity.
     (i) Do you agree? Give reasons for your opinion. (3)
     (ii) Give reasons why some people may disagree with you. (3)

                  (Total for Question 8 = 20 marks)

During the exam, remember to:
- ☑ plan your answers step by step
- ☑ use full sentences and good English
- ☑ spend 20 minutes on each question
- ☑ use the final 10 minutes of the exam to check everything through.

☑

If this had been the real exam, how well would you have done? Use the marking grid to check your progress. Answers to (a) appear on page 99, the grid for (b) is on page 25, the grid for (c) is on page 24 and the grid for (d) is on page 25.

Keyword glossary

baptism	confessing sins and being immersed in water as a sign of purification
blasphemy	associating oneself with God/language or deeds which insult God
the commandments	the collection of 10 laws given by God
confession	an acknowledgement or declaration of something
corban	a gift dedicated to God which meant that it could not be used for anything else
crucifixion	the Roman death penalty suffered by Jesus when he was nailed to the cross
disciples	followers of Jesus
Elijah	the Old Testament prophet believed to return before the Messiah
the eye of a needle	a metaphor used by Jesus to show that wealth makes it difficult to enter the Kingdom of God
fasting	going without food on certain days as a sign of devotion to God
Feast of Unleavened Bread	the first day of the Passover festival
Gethsemane	the place where Jesus was arrested
Golgotha	the place of the skull; the place where Jesus was crucified
healing miracle	a miracle in which Jesus shows his power over sickness
High Priest	the chief Jewish leader at the time of Jesus
Jairus	the synagogue ruler whose daughter was brought back to life by Jesus
John the Baptist	the man who baptized Jesus in the river Jordan
Judas Iscariot	the disciple who betrayed Jesus
the kingdom	the rule of God in people's lives
Last Supper	the last meal Jesus ate with his disciples which founded the Eucharist
the Law	the collection of laws handed down by God and collected in the Torah
Legion	a man from whom Jesus cast out many demons
Levi	a tax collector who was called to be a disciple
Messiah	the Anointed One (Christ) who would bring in God's Kingdom
Moses	the Old Testament prophet to whom God gave his laws

nature miracle	a miracle in which Jesus shows his power over nature
Palm Sunday	the Sunday before Good Friday when Jesus entered Jerusalem on a donkey
Passion	the sufferings of Jesus, especially in the time leading up to his crucifixion
Passover	Jewish festival celebrating the release from Egypt
Peter's denial	the way Peter said he was not a follower of Jesus after the arrest of Jesus
Pharisees	a religious group whose aim was to keep the traditional Jewish faith alive
Pontius Pilate	the Roman procurator (governor) of Judea at the time of Jesus
ritual cleanliness	the Jewish laws on food and washing which prevented anything unclean entering the body
Sabbath	the Jewish day of rest on the seventh day of the week
Sadducees	group of priests who controlled the Temple and collaborated with the Romans
Sanhedrin	the supreme Jewish council which found Jesus guilty of blasphemy
scribes	religious lawyers; originally men who made copies of the Torah
self-sacrifice	putting other people's needs before your own
service	an act of help or assistance
sinners	those who did not follow all the Jewish laws
Son of Man	a title used by Jesus of himself, probably meaning he would suffer before bringing in God's Kingdom
Sons of Zebedee	the brothers James and John whom Jesus called to follow him
the Temple	the building in Jerusalem where sacrifices were made
transfiguration	when Jesus' appearance was changed
true family	those who follow the teaching of Jesus
true greatness	the teaching of Jesus that service of others is true greatness
the Twelve	the twelve selected from the disciples to be Jesus' closest disciples
upper room	the place where the Last Supper took place